ALIENATION AND THE SOVIET ECONOMY

INDEPENDENT STUDIES IN POLITICAL ECONOMY:

AGRICULTURE AND THE STATE
Market Processes and Bureaucracy
E. C. Pasour, Jr.
Foreword by Bruce L. Gardner

ALIENATION AND THE SOVIET ECONOMY
The Collapse of the Socialist Era
Paul Craig Roberts
Foreword by Aaron Wildavsky

ANTITRUST AND MONOPOLY
Anatomy of a Policy Failure
D. T. Armentano
Foreword by Yale Brozen

ARMS, POLITICS AND THE ECONOMY
Historical and Contemporary Perspectives
Edited by Robert Higgs
Foreword by William A. Niskanen

FREEDOM, FEMINISM AND THE STATE
Edited by Wendy McElroy
Introduction by Lewis Perry

REGULATION AND THE REAGAN ERA
Politics, Bureaucracy and the Public Interest
Edited by Roger Meiners and Bruce Yandle
Foreword by Robert Crandall

TAXING ENERGY
Oil Severance Taxation and the Economy
Robert Deacon, Stephen DeCanio, H.E. Frech III, and M. Bruce Johnson
Foreword by Joseph P. Kalt

FORTHCOMING:

PRIVATE RIGHTS AND PUBLIC ILLUSIONS
Tibor Machan

THE ACADEMY AND THE STATE
Edited by John W. Sommer

LIBERTY AND CONSTITUTIONAL LAW
James L. Huffman

AMERICAN EDUCATION
The Private Challenge to Public Schools
Donald A. Erickson

*For further information on the Independent Institute's program
and a catalog of publications, please contact:*

THE INDEPENDENT INSTITUTE
134 Ninety-Eighth Avenue
Oakland, CA 94603
(415) 632-1366

ALIENATION AND THE SOVIET ECONOMY

The Collapse of the Socialist Era

With a New Introduction

PAUL CRAIG ROBERTS

Foreword by Aaron Wildavsky

INDEPENDENT STUDIES IN
POLITICAL ECONOMY

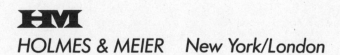

HOLMES & MEIER   *New York/London*

Published in the United States of America 1990 by
Holmes & Meier Publishers, Inc.
30 Irving Place
New York, NY 10003

Second edition © 1990 by The Independent Institute,
Oakland, CA

First edition © 1971 by Paul Craig Roberts,
published by University of New Mexico Press,
Albuquerque, NM

This book has been printed on acid-free paper.

Library of Congress Cataloging-in-Publication Data

Roberts, Paul Craig, 1939–
    Alienation and the Soviet economy : the collapse of the
  socialist era / Paul Craig Roberts : foreword by Aaron Wildavsky.—
Rev. ed.
        p.   cm.—(Independent studies in political economy)
    Includes bibliographical references and index.
        ISBN 0-8419-1247-5 (cl: acid-free paper). —ISBN 0-8419-1248-3
(pa: acid-free paper)
        1. Marxian economics.   2. Alienation (Social psychology)
    3. Soviet Union—Economic policy—1917–
        I. Title.   II. Series.
    HB97.5.R58   1990
    335.4'0947—dc20   90-5046
                                                            CIP

Manufactured in the United States of America

 The INDEPENDENT INSTITUTE

THE INDEPENDENT INSTITUTE is a nonprofit, scholarly research and educational organization which sponsors comprehensive studies on the political economy of critical social and economic problems.

The politicization of decision-making in society has largely confined debate to the narrow reconsideration of existing policies, the prevailing influence of partisan interests, and a stagnation of social innovation. In order to understand both the nature of and possible solutions to major public issues, the Independent Institute's studies adhere to the highest standards of independent inquiry and are pursued regardless of prevailing political or social biases and conventions. The resulting studies are widely distributed as books and other publications, and are publicly debated through numerous conference and media programs.

Through this uncommon independence, depth, and clarity, the Independent Institute pushes at the frontiers of our knowledge, redefines the debate over public issues, and fosters new and effective directions for government reform.

TO
MICHAEL POLANYI

Contents

Foreword

Why has the collapse of communism in the Soviet Union and Eastern Europe come upon us so unexpectedly? Why did our scholars and pundits and politicians not have the slightest inkling that anything so drastic and dramatic could occur? Why, if we understood according to our own capitalist precepts that command economies could not engage in sustained economic growth over time, did we so readily accept claims to the contrary?

Anxious not to underestimate their opponents, conservatives did not wish to play down Soviet and Soviet-satellite success. They would rather give the benefit of the doubt to greater growth lest they be in for nasty surprises. Liberals like to think of the Soviet economy as a poor cousin; it might not produce as much individual wealth or consumer satisfaction as ours but it could do well enough to demonstrate that there was a different, more collectivist mode of operation that could not be discounted. Belief in communist economic success was consistent with the liberals' belief in an expanding role for government in our own economy, so liberals gave the benefit of the doubt to the Soviets as well. In addition, there was the scholarly desire to be fair, not to put down another system because one disliked it or it was at odds with one's own country. Whether it was to aid defense budgets or to suggest there was no point in trying to out-compete the Soviet Union in armament, or just to demonstrate impartiality, the command economy was perceived to be a lot stronger than it was.

Each of these rationales drew strength from the fact that Soviet and Soviet-style economies did in fact grow. How could this be? The answer, scholars now know, is that a series of special factors lasting for some thirty years—a huge influx of workers (especially women) into the labor force, better technology than that of the 1930s, a huge increase in material inputs, and, in the 1970s, large foreign borrowings—caused temporary economic growth. Those few who adhered to fundamental principles of economics, like Roberts, saw that an economy based on production without profit could not succeed indefinitely.

It was readily assumed that the command economy had strengths of its own. In order to argue otherwise, one would have needed a great deal of confidence in fundamental principles. Such people are often called ideologues because they have pronounced views derived from adherence to fundamental theory. But pronounced views and fundamental principles are not necessarily wrong; they may be but they don't have to be wrong. Here, in Paul Craig Roberts's seminal book, we have perhaps the only scholarly effort to understand the relationship between Marxist theory and the Soviet economy that came out with a correct conclusion.

Who today would say that the Soviet Union or other communist nations have a centrally planned economy? No one plans to lose gross national product; no one plans to have worse health this year than the year before; no one intends to use two to three times more material or energy inputs than the capitalist economies, thereby becoming, in a swath through Eastern Europe, the most polluted nations on earth. Each and every communist country plans (or planned) to sacrifice current generations to its insatiable production fetish—more, more, more production is always better than less. But their belief was that their state would be better off in the future, however distant. They never meant inexorably to drive down the size of their economy so that the more they saved and invested the less their people would have; yet that is exactly what they did.

Before one can answer a question it must be posed accurately; specification of the phenomenon to be studied is essential to clear thinking. Yet Paul Craig Roberts had to struggle as late as 1971, when his *Alienation and the Soviet Economy* was published, to maintain this self-evident proposition.

Perhaps, it might be thought, a better formulation would be that the Soviet model is intended to mobilize resources for rapid industrialization, but not to manage the economy once developed. Not so. To his great credit, Roberts, a better student of Marx than many of Marx's followers, rescues the real meaning Marx gave to central planning. By showing what a political economy would have to be like to be centrally planned, Roberts reveals the immense distance between the communist economy as envisioned by Marx and the ersatz imitation of capitalism that Lenin introduced when he discovered that central planning was economically irrational. Trying to mimic capitalistic markets is not the same as abolishing them.

What gives Roberts the right to the book's title, and why does he feel it necessary to stress Marx's esoteric concept of "alienation" in a discussion of economics? Roberts gives the same answer Marx did, namely, that the alienation of man from work, from goods, from his mind and body, and from his social relations is caused by the market method of organizing production. The great thing Marx promised was not material wealth, for that he ascribed to capitalism. Indeed, Marx warned against attempting communism until capitalism, for all of its evils, had solved the problem of production so that there was abundance for all. Then and only then would communism, by abolishing market exchange, end alienation.

It would be hard to exaggerate Marx's anger over the way in which money and private property, in his opinion, hide the causes of alienation so that individuals are not merely exploited (given less than their economic due), but condemned to live with the false idea that enriching others at their expense is good for them. By making manifest the power relations in society and by granting power to the proletariat, by which Marx generally meant almost everyone except a few capitalists, alienation would be eliminated. It was not rapid industrialization, or military power, or any such material goal that Marx offered his followers. Roberts argues persuasively that "originally the purpose of central planning was to achieve the goal of a socialist society, that is, the abolition of the ills of capitalism by the elimination of commodity production." Since it was producing for exchange with money mediating relations among people that caused alienation, mankind would, as Californians say today, get in touch with their own feelings, i.e., end alienation by abolishing production for exchange.

A major reason why this Marxian thesis has been insufficiently recognized is that what Marx meant by socialism or communism acquired the name "war communism" after it failed and was abandoned. The special historical circumstances surrounding the civil war after the Bolshevik Revolution of 1917 encouraged the facile notion that war communism was a temporary expedient. Instead, Roberts reveals it to be the essence of socialism-communism, the real thing and not the fake that was substituted for it. That neither the fake nor the substitute work does not gainsay the fact that the real thing was tried because it was what Lenin and his associates believed was worth trying and not only because capitalists fled and other conditions made it convenient. By denying ourselves the knowledge of what Marx and Lenin really wanted, even if Lenin later decided it was better to give up that part of his ideals rather than risk the revolution on a failed economy, we in the Western democracies also denied ourselves the opportunity to understand Soviet-style systems as vulgar capitalism (that is, as capitalism without the things that make it work—markets, prices, profits, property) rather than as centrally planned. Thus the opportunity opened by Roberts and, before him, Michael Polanyi, to foresee the course of the Soviet economy, was lost. Surprise comes when we lack adequate theory. We have recently been surprised by the collapse of communist economies, because we rejected the intellectual path that would have brought us the necessary enlightenment.

The essence of war communism was for the government to seize food supplies from farmers in order to distribute them in kind to workers. (My father, who owned a dry goods store in Poltava in the Ukraine, experienced the other side of surplus appropriation when everything he had was taken away down to one chair to sit on.) The war, with its infamous "iron detachments," brutalized this confiscation but in essence it was exactly what Marx and Lenin wanted in that central authority replaced production of commodities for markets with governmentally organized production for direct use. The crux of Roberts's explanation is that

> Whatever the intention might be, in effect the primary function of the planning bureaucracy is to act as supply agents for enterprises in order to avoid free price formation and exchange on the market so that productive inputs will not have the appearance of commodities. This satisfies the ideology underlying the whole effort at the expense of notorious failures in supply.

The communist political economy is alienating in precisely Marx's sense in that it pretends to avoid the market while actually trying to embrace it without saying so, but succeeds in neither purpose. Who is living in a false mental world now?

In order to have genuine central planning, one would have to perform certain tasks for which central cognition is inappropriate. F. A. Hayek has publicized the inability of non-market economies to perform simultaneous calculations of supply and demand, or to make use of local knowledge producing adaptations to innumerable local conditions. Other inherent difficulties of central planning, which Roberts brings out, are equally applicable and perhaps more devastating. In an activity such as a national economy characterized by immense interdependencies, the effort of central planners to determine hierarchies of importance is hopeless. The whole point is that there isn't any one thing that is most important for everyone in every situation and under every condition. Efforts to provide substitutes for profit as a criterion of choice are, in Roberts's view, bound to fail. Now nearly two decades after he wrote, it is possible to locate eleven communist political economies in the world (China, North Korea, Vietnam, Cuba, the Soviet Union, East Germany, Bulgaria, Czechoslovakia, Poland, Rumania, Hungary). When people spend over forty years looking for something in many countries and do not find it, there is a good chance it is not there. Their preferred alternative is production, largely for its own sake. Other scholars have written volumes about the communist phenomenon of simultaneous shortages and surpluses, which Roberts disposes of in a throwaway clause: "Eventually there will be a shortage of storage space for production unrelated to wants."

So what do so-called central planners do in communist political economies? They wait and see what was done in the last few years and then add increments, usually up. Then they send down messages telling the actual producers to do more. But forecasts are presumably not plans. The incentive in Soviet-style systems is provided by the "success indicator," which says something about how many items are produced but nothing about their economic value. Would that most economists had understood earlier and better Roberts's view that "the major difference between the Soviet economy and the market economy lies in the rationality of the signals for managerial interpretation."

More than any other scholar of whom I am aware, including the major scholars of Marx's corpus, Paul Craig Roberts understood earlier and with greater intellectual power the nature of a Communist command economy whose commands cannot be obeyed. Looking at the Soviet economic system from the standpoint of his own model, he writes that "the economic reforms are not, as is generally believed, a matter of radical organizational change, but a matter of replacing signals that are less rational with signals that are more rational from the standpoint of economic efficiency." The truth of this, however, does not solve the cultural problem of a regime moving from bad economics to good economics when it has to shut itself down in the process. Many institutions and aspects of Soviet life, including de facto property rights, are dependent on the inefficient gross-output system of production.

Roberts could have made his pathbreaking book totally predictive if he had followed his logic to its full conclusion and concluded that communist economies cannot grow because they select the worst economic projects to subsidize the most, thereby violating the essential principle of economics. This is the best book to read on communist political economy for those who think they already know it all.

Aaron Wildavsky
Professor of Political Science
and Public Policy
University of California, Berkeley

Preface

The purpose of this book is to explain the operation of the Soviet economy in terms of its organizational principles and Marxian aspirations. I offer a conceptual framework that permits the Soviet economy to be understood as not centrally planned. And I show the impact on the operation of the Soviet economy of the original aspirations of Marxian socialism. This analysis is indebted to Michael Polanyi's seminal insights, which sovietologists have conscientiously ignored.

Sovietologists have been unanimous in classifying the Soviet economic system as centrally planned. With few exceptions, moreover, Alexander Gerschenkron's conclusion "that hardly anything in the momentous story of Soviet economic policies needs, or suffers, explanations in terms of its derivation from Karl Marx's economic theories"[1] is representative of prevailing opinion.

The analysis in this book supports the opposite classification and the opposite conclusion. It does not claim to be based primarily on new facts that I have discovered about the Soviet economy. I accept the main body of facts assembled by sovietologists and look at them through a different "window." The result is a systematic general treatment that is in itself both logically and historically consistent as well as consistent with the facts set forth by sovietologists. Instead of developing an ex post rationalization of these facts, this book traces the development and unfolding of a germinal idea as it moves from an abstract category into the consciousness of men and culminates in history.

1 Quoted from his Richard T. Ely Lecture at the 81st annual meeting of the American Economic Association, Chicago, 1968, published in the *American Economic Review, Papers and Proceedings*, May 1969, p. 16.

Acknowledgments

Few parts of this book are free of Michael Polanyi's influence. The thesis that the operation of the Soviet economy can be understood only as the outcome of the original Marxian aspirations is original with Polanyi and is asserted in "The Foolishness of History," *Encounter* (November 1957), and in "Towards a Theory of Conspicuous Production," *Soviet Survey* (October-December 1960). The analysis of organizational systems in terms of polycentricity is also original with Polanyi and is found in *The Logic of Liberty* (University of Chicago Press, 1951). At a time when scholarly judgment was distorted by a milieu of great hopes for planning, Polanyi saw the heart of the matter.

I am indebted to Matthew A. Stephenson who saw the significance and interest of my ideas connecting Marxian alienation to commodity production as soon as I mentioned them to him. He shares with me the responsibility for their development. Chapter 1 and the Appendix are based on the following papers by Roberts and Stephenson: "Alienation and Central Planning in Marx," *Slavic Review* (September 1968), "A Note on Marxian Alienation," *Oxford Economic Papers* (November 1970), and "The Concept of Alienation in Marx's *Capital*" (unpublished manuscript). Professor John Plamenatz read drafts of some of these papers, and a discussion we had influenced the form of Chapter 1.

My study of "war communism" was supported by the Relm Foundation and the American Philosophical Society and was first published in *Slavic Review* (June 1970). I am indebted to Dr. George Katkov for valuable discussions and aid in interpreting sources.

Many parts of this book have been either published in professional journals, presented at professional meetings, or tried on various faculties. The parts can be assessed independently, but each part is strengthened by its relationship to each of the others. They are brought together in this book because together they offer a general reformulation.

I am grateful to the editors of *Slavic Review, The Journal of Law and Economics, Oxford Economic Papers, Soviet Studies,* and *Public Choice* for permission to make use in this book of articles that I published in their pages. I am grateful to the *Journal of Political Economy* and the University of Chicago Press for permission to reprint part of my article, "Oskar Lange's Theory of Socialist Planning," © 1971 by the University of Chicago. Some of my arguments in Chapters 4 and 5 were first published in translation in Eastern Europe. Responses of Oxford dons and post-graduates to my Special University Lecture, January 20, 1969, were helpful.

I am indebted to Warren Nutter, my dissertation chairman at the University of Virginia, for his open-mindedness in allowing me to pursue my ideas. At another university at which I first expressed interest in the ideas developed in this book, I was confronted with a wall of dogmatism.

Various parts of this book have benefited at some stage in their formulation from comments by Warren Nutter, James M. Buchanan, Armen Alchian, R. H. Coase, Gordon Tullock, Edwin G. Dolan, and scholars who remain anonymous.

Introduction to the Revised Edition

I welcome the Independent Institute's initiative in sponsoring this new edition of *Alienation and the Soviet Economy*. The publication of this book two decades ago offered a new perspective on the Soviet economy. It is a perspective that scholars have found challenging, because it refutes both their explanation of Soviet economic history and their classification of the Soviet economy as planned. Following E. H. Carr and Maurice Dobb, scholars have denied that Marxism has been a force in Soviet economic history. Consequently, they have taken the concept of central economic planning out of its historical context and obscured its meaning. When Western scholars describe the Soviet economy as centrally planned, they do not mean the same thing as when Marx, Lenin, and Stalin used this term. To these revolutionaries, planning did not mean, as it generally means to modern writers, planning through markets or planning for industrialization. It meant the abolition of the market system.

This book treats Marxism seriously as a system of thought, and it explains Soviet economic history as a product of the interaction of Marxian intentions with a refractory reality. In my account, economic and historical necessities must make room for speculative excess as a force in history.

By 1971 when this book was first published, it was apparent to this author that reality had triumphed in the struggle with Marxism. But it was not until 1989 that Soviet leader Mikhail Gorbachev and *glasnost*, his policy permitting free expression, made this generally clear to the entire world.

To the West the collapse of communism was sudden and unexpected. It is disappearing before scholars ever understood its manifestations, and humankind is in danger of losing valuable lessons of its experience. Now that communist countries no longer exist, scholars no longer have to prove their objectivity by defending communism, and the republication of this book may help to save the lessons of a costly social experiment from oblivion.

In 1917 Lenin startled the Marxist world when he seized power in Russia in the name of a socialist proletariat. In the minds of most Marxists, Russia had not gone through the proper stages to be ripe for socialism, and so began debate and denunciation that to this day clutters up the field of Soviet studies.

To Marxists, Lenin appeared as an opportunist whose action flew in the face of the doctrine of historical materialism. According to this doctrine, the institutions and consciousness of men (ideology in the classical Marxian sense) in any historical period are determined by the economic organization of society. In Marx's words: "The mode of production of material life conditions the general process of social, political and intellectual life. It is not the consciousness of men that determines their existence, but their social existence that determines their consciousness."[1]

Lenin felt pressure to legitimize his seizure of power, and the doctrinal position that he took has been misinterpreted as an affirmation of the primacy of politics over economics—the reverse of historical materialism. Scholars concluded that in 1917 Lenin chose power over Marxian principle, and out of this mistaken interpretation of Lenin have come mistaken explanations of Soviet experience. The cumulative effect has been to downplay and deny the role of Marxian ideology. This denial had the effect of exonerating Marxism from any responsibility for the tyranny and brutalization of life in the Soviet Union, and this was, no doubt, an important unconscious motive of various authors.

It is clear from Lenin's *Collected Works* that at the time he seized power he did not consider this to be a disavowal of historical materialism. He accepted that man's consciousness—excepting a revolutionary vanguard as carrier of the program—is determined by the mode of production. Lenin thought that the Bolsheviks must change the mode of production into a socialist one if they were to remain in power. Otherwise, the Party would lose its grip due to the incompatibility of socialist rule with a bourgeois mode of production.

---

1. Karl Marx, A *Contribution to the Critique of Political Economy* (Chicago: Charles Kerr, 1904), pp. 11–12.

What did Lenin understand the bourgeois and socialist modes of production to be? He understood perfectly, as did Bukharin, Trotsky, and everyone else involved, Marx's writings about commodity production. They all understood that capitalism was a system of commodity production or production for exchange in the market. Producers are mutually independent, and production is separated from use by exchange. From these organizational characteristics follow capital, wage labor, the separation of value from price, economic crises, and alienation. Although each firm plans its own production, capitalist production as a whole is unplanned. The result is that man is pushed around by the forces of the market—forces of his own making. This, and not an emotional disaffection for work felt by laborers, is the meaning of *Marxian* alienation.[2]

Similarly, Marx's notion of freedom has nothing to do with the autonomy of the individual. "Freedom" is a term applied by Marx to a socialist society where conscious control has been established over social production and man is no longer subject to the blind forces of the market. Planned social production, as understood by Marx and Lenin, abolishes exchange altogether and establishes a direct unity of production with use.

In a Marxian planned economy there is no exchange between individual producers or between producers and consumers, no money, no private property, no economic crises, and no alienation. Planning of production for direct use, or what Stalin called products-exchange between town and country, emerges as the single defining organizational characteristic of Marxian socialism.

Having decided on the seizure of power, Lenin was committed to a transition to socialism. At first he seems to have had the idea of a transitional period based on the seizure of the banking system, but when nothing came of this he undertook a direct transition. This also failed, and Lenin was confronted with the requirements of theory and reality contradicting each other. By 1921 Lenin realized that his attempt to stamp out commodity production and establish socialist planning was a serious threat to the political survival of the Bolsheviks. Yet, he also believed that commodity production was itself a serious threat to the political survival of the Bolsheviks. Lenin frankly acknowledged the failure of his effort to establish socialist economic organization and the dilemma presented by the failure. He understood

2. This theme is developed in Chapter 1 of this book. For a complete exposition of Marx's economics, see Paul Craig Roberts and Matthew A. Stephenson, *Marx's Theory of Exchange, Alienation and Crisis* (Stanford, Calif.: Hoover Institution Press, 1973, republished in 1983 by Praeger Publishers).

failure to be a consequence of insufficient socialist consciousness among the population (particularly the peasants) and insufficient manufactured goods for distribution in kind to peasants in return for agricultural products.

There is some indication that Lenin and others were left with deeper doubts from the experience of war communism than were conveyed by this explanation of its failure. Some skepticism appeared about the possibility of a national economy operating without commercial principles, that is, without money, prices, profit, and markets.

Lenin died without resolving the dilemma presented by the failure of war communism: how to maintain a socialist political "superstructure" when the underlying mode of production was commodity production. His main line of reasoning seems to have been that the "superstructure" could be maintained for an unspecified period by Party control of the "commanding heights." During this period outputs would be increased to higher levels and a socialist consciousness instilled in the population. With outputs and consciousness at higher levels a second attempt to achieve socialist economic organization would be successful. This line of reasoning remained committed to socialism as a non-commodity form of production.

The New Economic Policy presented a fundamental problem. After all, according to Marxism commodity production is bourgeois production and engenders bourgeois consciousness. Whereas Lenin thought that a revolutionary vanguard could seize power as carrier of the program, he did not think that power could be maintained indefinitely unless the mode of production was transformed into a socialist one.

Stalin revived the effort to establish a non-commodity mode of production. His view that the problem with collective farms was their commodity relation to the state suggests that he saw the functions of planning in terms of (1) the establishment of a non-commodity mode of production in the state (socialist) sector, that is, within industrial production, and (2) the rapid increase in industrial production so that this mode of production could be extended to agriculture and commodity relations brought to an end. Like Lenin, Stalin concluded that socialist economic organization could not be achieved throughout the economy until industrial production reached higher levels. The more rapid the growth, the sooner socialist economic organization could be achieved.

Over time, the impossibility of achieving a non-commodity form of production in a complex economy has produced sufficient frustration and economic irrationality to weaken and undermine the ideological program for the economy. Today the system of material supply is an institutional legacy of forgotten or vaguely understood aspirations. In the ruins of the ideological program to transform man by transforming the basis for relations among men lives a bureaucratic vested interest. But too much has to be disregarded to find the origins of planning in a bureaucratic vested interest or in a need for a strong military to defend and extend the boundaries of socialism. Lenin, of course, did understand planning as a defense of socialism—but he saw it as a protection that followed from eliminating bourgeois consciousness by establishing a non-commodity mode of production.

In the Soviet Union, there have been no legal markets for industrial materials, and the planning apparatus has directed its efforts into supplying firms in lieu of their provisioning themselves through markets. The primary function of the planning bureaucracy has been to act as supply agent for enterprises. These efforts are ideological in origin. Free price formation and exchange in the market must be avoided so that productive inputs within the state sector do not have the character of commodities. If, as I argue, the supply apparatus cannot perform its formal hierarchic function and must function informally and polycentrically by directing its activities toward overcoming problems created by its own existence, then commodity production has not been transcended but has acquired an abstract and irrational form. The heroic efforts, now largely traditional but once fiercely ideological, have succeeded only in avoiding the *appearance* of commodity production in the state sector. As the Soviets themselves realize, by abandoning planning they are abandoning economic irrationality. For example, Vasili Selyunin wrote in *Komsomolskaya Pravda* on January 17, 1990, that "plans have nothing to do with real life."

In the Soviet Union the heirs of a revolution which attempted to achieve socialist economic organization that would be superior productively and morally to private property, today acknowledge the superiority of private property and market incentives and demand their restoration. The Marxian goal of replacing commodity production with central economic planning seems absurd to modern Soviet economists, who, instead, attribute the problems of the Soviet economy to the absence of commodity production. For example, in an interview with *Sotsialisticheskaya Industria* on December 12, 1989, Yaroslav Kuzminov said that "essentially, we are not a commodity production system, and it is for this reason that we do not have the elements of a developed market economy: A market of commodities, manpower, and capital."

The new Soviet law permitting private property and the repudiation on February 7, 1990, of Article 6 of the Soviet constitution which had granted the Communist Party a monopoly on political power mark the end of the Marxist era. This book explains the goals of this era and why they failed. If we do not learn the lessons, the twentieth century will have been lived in vain.

Paul Craig Roberts
Washington, D.C.

ALIENATION AND THE SOVIET ECONOMY

CHAPTER 1

Alienation and Central Planning in Marx

The publication in 1932 of the *Economic and Philosophical Manuscripts* (1844) has resulted in many attempts to reinterpret and reformulate Marx. The concept of alienation, the central theme of the *Manuscripts*, seems to many to cast Marxism in an altogether new light. The surprise and controversy generated from finding a second Marx, or another and different aspect of Marx, reflect only a prevalent neglect of the logical structure of the programmatic content of Marx's work. The interpretations of Marxian alienation that have resulted from the study of the *Manuscripts* also reflect this neglect and have not led to any real progress in understanding Marx. If anything, the interpretations have lessened our understanding of Marx by raising the paradox of two separate Marxes—a young Marx and a mature Marx—and have encouraged a tendency by scholars to dismiss Marx as wildly inconsistent.

This chapter presents an interpretation of Marxian alienation that demonstrates the consistency of Marx's general scheme and the logic of the programmatic implications of his work. In this programmatic logic are the aspirations that were the cause of the Bolsheviks' economic policies during the "war communism" period. This is the route by which we will follow an abstract idea as it moves into the consciousness of men and culminates in history. The interpretation of Marxian alienation developed here also allows reconciliation of widely split opinion among knowledgeable scholars, because it is an interpretation consistent with Marx's self-image as the Scientific

1

Socialist and, thereby, establishes continuity between the young and the mature Marx.

Our interpretation finds the source of alienation in the "commodity mode of production" by which Marx means the market system. Unlike psychological and sociological approaches from which alienation is studied from the personal standpoint of the individual, the approach here is to look for the cause of alienation in the mode of production, i.e., in the method of economic organization. This approach to Marxian alienation is appropriate, given Marx's materialist conception of history in which the institutions and consciousness of men (ideology in the classical Marxian sense) in any historical period are determined by the economic organization of society. In Marx's words:

> The mode of production in material life determines the general character of the social, political and spiritual processes of life. It is not the consciousness of men that determines their existence, but on the contrary, their social existence determines their consciousness.[1]

Although alienation is not the terminology in *Capital*,[2] this chapter will show that Marx views alienation as an inherent characteristic of commodity production—the method of economic organization in a market system. It is his pre-analytic vision of society upon which his theoretical analysis in *Capital* is built.

To put our interpretation of Marxian alienation into perspective (see Appendix), other interpretations that find the source of Marxian alienation in private property, the division of labor, and greed are critically analyzed. It is shown that existing alternative interpreta-

1. Karl Marx, *A Contribution to the Critique of Political Economy* (Chicago: Charles Kerr, 1904), pp. 11-12.
2. The term "alienation" is not altogether absent in *Capital*. In volume III the term appears in the sense in which it is interpreted in this chapter: "the relationship of capital actually conceals the inner connection behind the utter indifference, isolation, and alienation in which [the laborer is placed] vis-a-vis the means incorporating his labour" (Karl Marx, *Capital*, vol. III, New York: International Publishers, 1967, p. 85).
Marx probably dropped the term "alienation" because (1) the concept was being adopted by socialist groups that were rivals and (2) for most people the term had "idealistic" connotations that Marx did not accept and that were inconsistent with his doctrine of historical materialism. On these points see Oscar J. Hammen, 'The Young Marx Reconsidered," *Journal of the History of Ideas*, vol. XXXI, no. 1 (1970), pp. 109-20.

tions either cannot account for the uniqueness of Marxian alienation to capitalism, the critique of which is Marx's major work, or they do not take into account the materialist conception of history which is, as Tucker himself states, the matrix of Marx's thought.[3]

Alienation

In the manuscript "Alienated Labor," Marx specifically denotes four aspects of man's alienation. First, there is the alienation of man from the product of his labor. The product of labor dominates man and not vice versa.[4] It has an existence independent of man as something alien to him and becomes a power that confronts him.

Second, man is alienated from labor itself, i.e., from productive activity.[5] Work becomes an activity that is external to, and independent of, the worker and an activity in which the worker finds no fulfillment. A worker does not produce use-value for himself but exchange-value. "The external character of work for the worker is shown by the fact that it is not his own work but work for someone else, that in work he does not belong to himself but to another person."[6] The results of his own activity accrue to him only in his leisure; in what should be the most human of all activity—work—he is alienated.

Marx infers a third characteristic of alienated labor from the preceding two. Alienated labor results in man being alienated from himself, his own body, his external nature, his mental life, and his human life.[7] Man's "life activity"—his labor—appears only as a means to satisfy his needs, that is, to make a living. But a man's work is his life; therefore, "life itself appears only as a means of life."[8]

Marx finds the fourth characteristic, that man is alienated from other men, to be a direct consequence of the other three. "What is true of man's relationship to his work, to the product of his work and to himself, is also true of his relationship to other men, to their labor and to the objects of their labor."[9]

3. Robert C. Tucker, *Philosophy and Myth in Karl Marx* (Cambridge: Cambridge University Press, 1961), p. 23.

4. Karl Marx, *Economic and Philosophical Manuscripts*, translated by T. B. Bottomore, reprinted in Erich Fromm, *Marx's Concept of Man* (New York: Frederick Ungar, 1961), pp. 96-97.

5. Ibid., pp. 98-99.   6. Ibid., p. 99.   7. Ibid., p. 103.
8. Ibid., p. 101.   9. Ibid., p. 103.

Embodiment of Alienation in Commodity Production

Marx defines a commodity as an object which is produced by human labor for the purpose of exchange.[10] An object produced for an individual's own consumption possesses use-value for the individual, but since it is not produced for the purpose of exchange, it is not a commodity. "All commodities are non-use-values for their owners [producers], and use-values for their non-owners [consumers]."[11]

Commodities acquire their relations as values through exchange.[12] Exchange is also the act whereby producers come into social contact with one another. "The persons exist for one another merely as representatives of, and therefore, as owners of commodities."[13] Thus, for Marx, exchange is an act whereby human beings acting as mutually independent persons confront one another in the sale of commodities.[14]

This is not Webster's definition of exchange, and one should beware of attaching standard definitions to the terms that Marx used. After elaborating his concept of exchange, Marx shows that historically there have been a number of societies in which the "swap" of goods and services among the members of the community did not constitute exchange and that, therefore, these goods are not, by definition, commodities. For example, a patriarchal family, a feudal manor, an ancient Indian commune, or the Inca State in Peru did not, according to Marx, include or permit mutual independence of human beings and exchange relationships (market relationships). As Marx succinctly put it: "Commodity exchange begins where community life ends."[15]

In a market system the specific, concrete labor of an individual worker is manifested as a part of the labor of society, that is, it acquires a social character (and becomes abstract general labor) only through the act of exchange. But the act of exchange establishes only indirectly the social relationships between individuals at work. The

10. Karl Marx, *Capital*, vol. I (Modern Library; New York: Random House, 1906), chap. 1.
11. Ibid., p. 97.   12. Ibid.   13. Ibid., pp. 96-97.
14. Karl Marx, *Capital*, vol. I (Everyman's Library; London: J. M. Dent, 1957), p. 63.
15. Ibid.

direct relation in exchange is between things (commodities). The fact that exchange establishes indirectly the social relationship between individuals by establishing a direct relation between commodities is apparent to everyone until exchange becomes so varied and complex that a special commodity—money—evolves as the universal equivalent by which the value of all other commodities can be measured. Marx says that it is "just this ultimate money form of the world of commodities that actually conceals, instead of disclosing the social character of private labor and the social relations between individual producers."[16]

In advanced stages of commodity production, the social relationships of individual producers are hidden by the veil of money. What appears is a world of mutually independent human beings who fulfill their needs through the impersonal mechanism of the market. Thus, the veil of money or commodities, by hiding the actual social relationships, projects a false consciousness and screens the phenomenon of exploitation.[17]

The fetishism of commodities, by hiding the actual social relationships, prevents men from knowing the objective reality;[18] for example, men are unaware of exploitation. Marx is more indignant that the veil blinds men to exploitation than over the exploitation itself. It is not exploitation that is unique to capitalism but the blindness to it. The blindness to exploitation is one aspect of the false consciousness resulting from commodity production: "This fetishism of commodities has its origin . . . in the peculiar social character of the labor that produces them."[19] As we shall show, the peculiar social character of the labor which produces commodities is alienated labor; and this directly connects the veiling of objective reality, alienated labor, and commodity production.

16. Marx, *Capital*, vol. I (Modern Library), p. 87.
17. "A man who has a direct obligation to another, as a serf does to a master, knows directly the source of power over him. But one who sells his labor power for money may feel himself to be free. The product of the laborer can thus be easily 'abstracted' into money and, through the exchange system, be 'abstracted' from him." Daniel Bell, *The End of Ideology* (Glencoe: the Free Press, 1960), p. 341. Cf. Paul M. Sweezy, *The Theory of Capitalist Development* (New York: Monthly Review Press, 1964), p. 39. Cf. Marx, *Capital*, vol. I (Modern Library), p. 89.
18. Marx, *Capital*, vol. I (Modern Library), p. 83. Cf. Sweezy, *Theory of Capitalist Development*, pp. 34-40.
19. Marx, *Capital*, vol. I (Modern Library), p. 83.

Herein lies Marx's mature treatment of alienation. Man is dominated by an incorrect image of his world. The ideology (in the classical Marxian sense) resulting from the commodity mode of production causes man to perceive the market system as a force beyond his control to which he must adjust. He accepts the market mode of life as unquestionable. Such a perception prevents man from living in the world in a fashion that is otherwise possible for him. It is an alienation that he does not consciously experience but which keeps him from "real positive science" and thereby from establishing conscious social control over economic life and controlling his own destiny. Destruction of the system of commodity production destroys the veil or false consciousness that blinds man to the power within his grasp to fashion his own history. Man is alienated because his economic life, which according to Marx determines his social and political institutions and consciousness, has control over him.[20]

In his discussion of commodity fetishism, Marx develops the theme that in the act of exchange the social relations between men

20. That man's economic life has control over him is not a complaint that man is subservient to necessity but a complaint that man is subservient to productive relations that are of his own making. Marx accepts necessity as a fact of economic life "in all forms of society and under all possible modes of production." He writes:

In fact the realm of freedom does not commence until the point is passed where labor under the compulsion of necessity and of external utility is required. In the very nature of things it lies beyond the sphere of material production in the strict meaning of the term. Just as the savage must wrestle with nature, in order to satisfy his wants, in order to maintain his life and reproduce it, so civilized man has to do it, and he must do it in all forms of society and under all possible modes of production. With his development the realm of natural necessity expands, because his wants increase; but at the same time the forces of production increase, by which these wants are satisfied. Freedom in this field can consist only of the fact that socialized man, the associated producers, regulate their interchange with nature rationally, bring it under their common control, instead of being ruled by it as by some blind power; that they accomplish their task with the least expenditure of energy and under conditions most adequate to their human nature and most worthy of it. But it always remains a realm of necessity. Beyond it begins that development of human power which is its own end, the true realm of freedom, which, however, can flourish only upon that realm of necessity as its basis. The shortening of the working day is its fundamental prerequisite (Karl Marx, *Capital*, vol. III, Chicago: Charles Kerr, 1909, pp. 954-55).

This passage makes clear that Marx does not conceive of overcoming alienation in terms of transcending economic necessity or scarcity. By "that development of human power which is its own end, the true realm of freedom" he means artistic creativity. The less time that man must give each day to providing his food, clothing, housing, transportation, and other economic necessities, the more of that day he can spend in "the true realm of freedom," that is, in artistic expression for its own sake.

assume "the fantastic form of a relation between things."[21] Some
have noted that there is a connection between the fetishism of commodities and alienation,[22] but the connection generally is not explored. The fourth aspect of alienation, noted previously as the
alienation of man from his fellow men, is that aspect most obviously
seen in Marx's concept of commodity fetishism. In the marketplace
human bonds of family, friendship, and community do not exist;
individuals face one another solely as owners of commodities.

Since it is our purpose to discover the relationship between all
aspects of alienation and commodity production, it is necessary to
look beyond Marx's discussion of commodity fetishism to consider
the relationship among commodities, the labor that produces them,
and alienated labor. In *A Contribution to the Critique of Political
Economy*, Marx discusses the characteristics of labor that produce
commodities. Labor that produces commodities is labor devoid of
any quality. The individuality of labor is lost, and the specific forms
of labor are lost in their abstraction into money. Labor that produces
commodities is labor that creates exchange-value instead of use-value
for the laborer.[23] And, finally, labor that produces commodities is
"characterized by the fact that even the social relations of men appear
in the reversed form of a social relation of things."[24]

Man is alienated from the objects of his labor, the work process,
and from his own being when his labor loses its quality and individuality and when his labor is expended in producing for the market.
Man is alienated from other men when his labor results in the personification of objects. Clearly, labor that creates commodities is
alienated labor.

These characteristics of the labor that produces commodities are
revealed in the antitheses and contradictions which, in *Capital*,
Marx finds to be inherent in commodities. In commodities are "the
antithesis between use-value and [exchange-]value; the contradiction
involved in the fact that individual labor must simultaneously
manifest itself as directly social labor, the contradiction involved in

21. Marx, *Capital*, vol. I (Modern Library), p. 83.
22. See, for example, Igor S. Kon, "The Concept of Alienation in Modern Sociol-
ogy," *Social Research*, vol. XXXIV, no. 3 (autumn 1967), pp. 507-28.
23. Marx, *Critique of Political Economy*, pp. 24-27.
24. Ibid., p. 30.

the fact that particular concrete labor only counts as abstract general labor; the antithesis between the personification of objects and representation of persons by things."[25]

The various aspects of alienation given in the *Economic and Philosophical Manuscripts* are immanent in the nature of commodities. The contradictions and antitheses present in commodities, which are analyzed in *Capital*, are manifestations of alienation. The alienation of man from the product of his labor, from the work process itself, from his own being, and from other men is manifested in the contradictions between use-value and exchange-value, individual labor and social labor, particular concrete labor and abstract general labor, and the personification of objects and representation of persons by things—all contradictions being inherent features of commodity production.

It is possible, perhaps, to pair single aspects of alienation with single contradictions immanent in a commodity. As pointed out, others have noticed the connection between the alienation of man from his fellows and commodity fetishism, which in the terminology of *Capital* is "the antithesis between the personification of objects and the representation of persons by things."

The contradiction between use-value and exchange-value implies the alienation of man from the objects of his own labor. Use-value is realized when man produces directly for himself, his family, or his community; exchange-value is realized when man produces for the impersonal market. The specific products of a man's work accrue to other (unknown) men.

The contradictions between individual labor and social labor and between specific concrete labor and abstract general labor imply the alienation of man from the work process. Marx says that labor creating exchange-value (commodities) is abstract general labor. From the viewpoint of the market it is immaterial who the individual worker is or whether he is a tailor, a carpenter, or a manager. The specific concrete character of labor is lost by its abstraction into money.[26]

The alienation of man from his own being follows from his alienation from the product of his labor and the work process. According to Marx, since man realizes himself in work, alienation from the

25. Marx, *Capital*, vol. I (Everyman's Library), p. 92.
26. Marx, *Critique of Political Economy*, pp. 24-25.

products of his work and from productive activity results in alienation from his own being.

It is possible to jump to the conclusions that by "alienation of man from the objects of his own labor" Marx meant that the worker's product was expropriated by the capitalist and that by "alienation from the work process" Marx meant that the worker suffered under the monotony of the assembly line. These are the conclusions to which some have come. However, having found alienation to be an inherent feature of commodity production, Marx proceeded to analyze "scientifically" the development of the capitalistic system. The contradictions and antitheses of that system, which Marx found revealed in such phenomena as crises, follow directly from the contradictions and antitheses immanent in commodity production, which in turn are manifestations of the various aspects of alienation. Although Marx made many references to the worker's plight, *Capital* is not a study of the psychological and sociological features of alienation. Since Marxian alienation is a feature of a particular mode of production, it was the study of that mode of production which was the major work of his life.

To summarize, we have argued that since labor that creates commodities is alienated labor, the contradictions in the relations of production of commodities can be expected to reflect the characteristics of alienated labor. In the *Manuscripts* Marx gives the characteristics of alienated labor. In the *Critique of Political Economy* and in *Capital* he gives the characteristics of labor that produces commodities. We see that the characteristics of labor that produces commodities are the characteristics of alienated labor and conclude that commodities are produced by alienated labor. In *Capital*, Marx gives the contradictions inherent in the commodity mode of production. We see that these contradictions are manifestations of alienation and conclude that Marxian alienation is embodied in the phenomenon of commodity production.

Transcendence of Alienation

To Marx, commodity production reaches its highest stage of development in modern capitalism. Although ancient and feudal societies experienced a foretaste of commodity production, it was not the principal mode of production during those times. Except perhaps in some nascent commercial centers, man's relation to his work and to other men was convivial rather than commercial.

Marx's interpretation of alienation is unique in that he sees the phenomenon as being the product of the developed market system. The method of economic organization enslaves both workers and capitalists. The unique character of Marxian alienation permits a unique solution. Organization of autonomous producers in a system of market relationships is replaced by uniting the whole of society into a single factory.[27] The goal was to transcend Marxian alienation by transforming economic organization and providing a new basis for relations between men. Upon this new basis a new society would arise.

We are not positing the truth of alienation or claiming that central economic planning actually would eliminate alienation.[28] We are merely saying that in the Marxian scheme, central planning eliminates Marxian alienation by eliminating the exchange relationships of commodity production, that is, we are merely offering an interpretation of Marx. Consistent with his dictum that it was unscientific to discuss the way in which future society would function, Marx never gave the blueprint of how man would establish conscious control over the "material life-process." However, Marx was not in doubt that the change in consciousness that would give man self-realization and freedom in communist society would result from a profound change in the relations of production. Economic life would no longer be autonomous as in the market system.

This theme is found throughout his writings. In The German Ideology Marx writes that

Communism differs from all previous movements in that it overturns the basis of all earlier relations of production and intercourse, and for the first time consciously treats all natural premises as the creatures of men, strips them of their natural character and subjugates them to the

27. As Lenin expresses it in State and Revolution (New York: Little Lenin Library, 1932), "The whole of society will have become one office and one factory" (p. 84).
28. The possibility that the concept of Marxian alienation might be only a rationale for Marx's hatred of capitalism does not invalidate our interpretation of Marxian alienation. Whether or not Marx was sincere in his concern with alienation is not relevant to our interpretation of his concept of alienation.

power of individuals united. Its organization is, therefore, essentially economic, the material production of the conditions of this unity; it turns existing conditions into conditions of unity. The reality, which communism is creating, is precisely the real basis for rendering it impossible that anything should exist independently of individuals, in so far as things are only a product of the preceding intercourse of individuals themselves.[29]

In *The Civil War in France*, Marx describes communism as a system under which "united cooperative societies are to regulate the national production under a common plan, thus taking it under their own control and putting an end to the constant anarchy and periodical convulsions which are the fatality of capitalist production."[30] In the first volume of *Capital*, Marx says that "the life-process of society, which is based on the process of material production, does not strip off its mystical veil until it is treated as production by freely associated men, and is consciously regulated by them in accordance with a settled plan."[31] In the third volume of *Capital*, Marx says that under communism cooperative efforts will be unified by "one commanding will, and this performs a function, which does not refer to fragmentary operations, but to the combined labor of the workshop, in the same way as does that of a director of an orchestra."[32] He says that even under communism man must work for his living and that freedom in economics "can consist only of the fact that socialized man, the associated producers, regulate their interchange with nature rationally, bring it under their common control, instead of being ruled by it as by some blind power."[33] The theme is pervasive that under communism purposive social control takes the place of the autonomy of the market system.

This theme in Marx is consistent with his materialistic conception of history. The inevitable change from autonomous commodity production to conscious planning frees man from an illusory and false

29. Marx, *The German Ideology* (New York: International Publishers, 1968), p. 70.
30. Marx, *The Civil War in France* in Marx and Engels, *Basic Writings on Politics and Philosophy*, edited by Lewis S. Feuer (New York: Doubleday Anchor Book, 1959), p. 370.
31. Marx, *Capital*, vol. I (Modern Library), p. 92.
32. Marx, *Capital*, vol. III (Charles Kerr, 1909), p. 451.
33. Ibid., p. 954.

consciousness and ends his alienation. Just as in Feuerbach religion is the veil that keeps man from reality, in Marx commodity production is the veil that blinds man to the power that is within his grasp to control his own life: "Just as, in the sphere of religion, man is dominated by the creature of his own brain; so in the sphere of capitalist production, he is dominated by the creature of his own hand."[34]

In a socialist society the labor-power of individual producers is consciously applied as the combined labor-power of the community.[35] There is an analogue between the role of the individual producer in a patriarchal society and his role in a socialist society. In a patriarchal society the labor of the individual is viewed as a portion of the labor of the family; in a socialist society the labor of the individual is viewed as a portion of the labor of the community. Use-values for either the family or the community are produced, but commodities are not produced. Since in a socialist society the total product of the community is a social product, a means of distribution must be devised. Marx says that "distribution will vary with the productive organization of the community and the degree of historical development attained by the producers," but suggests as an example "that the share of each individual producer in the means of subsistence is determined by his labour-time."[36] Also, the apportionment of labor time "in accordance with a definite social plan maintains the proper proportion between the different kinds of work to be done and the various wants of the community."[37] With such a social plan commodity production is eliminated.

Marx's idea that commodity production would be replaced by planning under socialism became an integral part of socialist thought. According to Engels, when society gains possession of the means of production, the social relationships between producers will change fundamentally. Products will no longer enter into social use through exchange. "People will be able to manage everything very simply, without the intervention of the famous 'value.' "[38]

34. Marx, *Capital*, vol. I (Everyman's Library), p. 685.
35. Marx, *Capital*, vol. I (Modern Library), p. 90.
36. Ibid.   37. Ibid.
38. Frederick Engels, *Anti-Dühring* (New York: International Publishers, 1966), p. 338.

In a similar vein, Nikolai Bukharin wrote in *The Economics of the Transitional Period*: "Indeed, as soon as we deal with an organized national economy, all the basic 'problems' of political economy, such as price, value, profit, etc., simply disappear. Here 'relations between men' are no longer expressed as 'relations between things,' for here the economy is regulated not by the blind forces of the market and competition, but by the consciously carried out plan. . . . The end of capitalist and commodity society signifies the end of political economy."[39]

It is unquestionable that the Marxian vision of economic systems was the Bolshevik vision. The first section of the first chapter of Bukharin's *The ABC of Communism* is entitled "Commodity Economy," which he concludes: "WE SEE, THEREFORE, THAT THE PRIMARY CHARACTERISTIC OF THE CAPITALIST SYSTEM IS A COMMODITY ECONOMY; THAT IS, AN ECONOMY WHICH PRODUCES FOR THE MARKET."

The writings of Lenin also show that the elimination of commodity production was an objective to be realized by the organization of the Soviet economy. In *State and Revolution* Lenin says: "Every member of society, performing a certain part of socially-necessary work, receives a certificate from society that he has done such and such a quantity of work. According to this certificate, he receives from the public warehouses, where the articles of consumption are stored, a corresponding quantity of products."[40]

The parallel to (or paraphrasing of) Marx is clear: "In the case of socialized production, the money-capital is eliminated. Society distributes labor-power and means of production to the different lines of occupation. The producers may eventually receive paper checks, by means of which they withdraw from the social supply of means of consumption a share corresponding to their labor-time. These checks are not money. They do not circulate."[41]

The use of such certificates or paper checks eliminates the role of money as the medium in which exchange-values are established.

39. Quoted in Adam Kaufman, "The Origin of the Political Economy of Socialism," *Soviet Studies*, vol. IV, no. 3 (January 1953), p. 245.
40. Lenin, *State and Revolution*, p. 84.
41. Marx, *Capital*, vol. II, translated by E. Untermann (Chicago: Charles Kerr, 1907), p. 412.

These certificates are requisitions to a stock room and are the means by which the products of a society that is now united into a single factory are distributed. According to Marxian socialists, economic planning replaces a system of exchange relations and renders irrelevant the law of value. Sweezy states the point clearly: "It follows that in so far as the allocation of productive activity is brought under conscious control, the law of value loses its relevance and importance; its place is taken by the principle of planning. In the economics of a socialist society the theory of planning should hold the same basic position as the theory of value in the economics of a capitalist society. Value and planning are as much opposed, and for the same reasons, as capitalism and socialism."[42]

Though explicitly or implicitly denied by most writers, it is documented in the following chapter that the program of action of war communism represented a conscious attempt to establish socialist organization. Thus, the first action of revolutionary socialists in power reflected the intellectual ideas and moral intentions of their heritage. The emergence of ruin rather than utopia from the effort to eliminate commodity production is the reason why there has never been a second Soviet attempt to eliminate commodity production wholesale.

Western observers of the Soviet Union have seen central economic planning as a device for achieving rapid industrialization, high rates of economic growth, military power, and similar goals. It is not denied that these are some of the goals of the Soviet Union, but these are ex post goals. Originally the purpose of central planning was to achieve the goal of a socialist society, that is, the abolition of the ills of capitalism by the elimination of commodity production.

The idea of central planning grew out of the merging of the socialists' desire to abolish the system of commodity production with the belief that man, by the application of science to the study of society, could shape and direct society in any manner he wished.[43] To fail to see central planning in the Soviet Union as an attempt to eliminate commodity production is a denial of the power of Marx's thought in shaping the course of human events.

42. Sweezy, *Theory of Capitalist Development*, pp. 53-54.
43. As expressed by Engels in *Anti-Dühring* (International Publishers), socialist men "with full consciousness, will fashion their own history" (p. 310).

Marx's Classification of Economic Systems

It has been necessary to develop systematically and generally the relationship of Marxian alienation to commodity production because it is one of the foundations of the thesis of this book. This relationship has aspects which could be explored further,[44] but our primary concern is with the implications of this relationship in the classification of economic systems. By drawing on the previous analysis and setting out formally the Marxian classification of economic systems, we can lay the foundation for relating the analysis of intellectual ideas in Chapter 1 to the organizational theory of Chapter 3 in which the classification of economic systems in terms of polycentricity and hierarchy is shown to be organizationally synonymous with Marx's classification in terms of commodity and non-commodity. This will allow the Soviet economic system to be analyzed in Chapter 4 both in terms of theoretical organizational principles and Marxian aspirations.

Marx classifies economic systems according to the mode of production that predominates. For Marx there are only two general modes of production: commodity production and production for direct

44. One important aspect relates to the study of economic history. In "The Pirenne Thesis: Towards Reformulation" I argue that "it is justified to study economic history with a view to the presence of different combinations of the functional [non-commodity] and the commercial [commodity] methods of organization in order to assess the dominating influence, arising out of the conflict between the convivial existence of custom and impersonal commercialism, upon social and economic organization (and on intellectual history, e.g., Socialism)," and I interpreted European economic history as the modification of a largely custom-bound economic system "by continuous stages towards a market system, with the various intermediate forms offering different combinations of functional and commercial rationality" (Classica et Mediaevalia, vol. XXV, 1964, p. 313). Afterwards I realized that my perspective was congruous with Marx's and Engels's vision of economic history. Engels states that "the commodity form and money penetrate the internal economy of the community directly associated for production; they break one tie after another within the community and dissolve the community into a mass of private producers" (Anti-Dühring, International Publishers, p. 339). I then realized that the primary thesis of Marx was not one of private property and exploitation but that under the commodity mode of production there is a separation between the process of production and use that is bridged only by commercial principles, the result being the (Marxian) alienation of man.

The non-commodity character of pre-capitalist economic systems is set out by Marx in Pre-Capitalist Economic Formations (New York: International Publishers, 1969) in which there is study of various historical forms of the non-commodity mode of production. This approach to economic history is fundamental, and has been revived by Karl Polanyi and his students.

use. Marx's classification is both theoretically and historically interesting. Historically there have been many societies in which production for direct use by the family or community was dominant but, according to Marx, whether production is for direct use by the community or for direct use by a feudal lord or a ruling class, in all societies prior to capitalistic ones production was predominantly for direct use.

According to Marx the division of labor characterizes human existence and cannot be transcended, although its deleterious effects can be mitigated under communism.[45] Division of labor is, therefore, a characteristic of all economies. Figure 1 represents the set of all

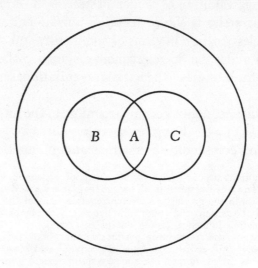

A—division of labor element
B—production for direct-use element
C—production for sale element

FIGURE 1.

45. Marx says that under communism man is able to avoid deleterious effects of the division of labor while maintaining the social division of labor because "society regulates the general production and thus makes it possible for me to do one thing today and another tomorrow" (German Ideology, p. 22).

characteristics of economies. Any element or point is a single characteristic of some economy or economies. All economies must include
point A. For Marxian theoretical taxonomy, any economy must include points A and B but not C (production for direct use), or points
A and C but not B (commodity production). Both market capitalism and market socialism are commodity production economies.
They share in common a mode of production (i.e., basic economic
organization) and some private property rights (e.g., labor) but differ
in most property arrangements (in terms of formal ownership).
Among the production for direct-use economies are found ritual
(primitive and feudal) economies and Marx's vision of the planned
socialist economy. They share in common production for direct use
and some elements of tradition but differ in the exercise of conscious
will over economic life. In Marx's historical classification, as compared to a purely theoretical classification, economies may exist that
possess elements B and C because historically the commodity mode
grew out of a non-commodity mode; the market system developed
out of peripheral trade, and there is still some production for direct
use in the capitalist economy.

Whether treated purely theoretically or historically, Marx's classification of economic systems is in terms of their *organizational*
structures. In this, Marx is sound. His life work is a study of capitalist
production, and he succeeded in defining capitalist production in
terms of its unique property. It is not private property, division of
labor, and surplus-labor that are unique to capitalism but production
for exchange on the market as the dominant mode of production.

The mode of production, i.e., the method of economic organization, is the source for the rationality of the division of labor. In the
commodity mode of production, the division of labor receives its rationality through market exchange. In a non-commodity mode of
production, the division of labor receives its rationality through social
custom as in a ritual economy or through a social plan as in communism. Marx explicitly states that the "division of labor is a necessary condition for the production of commodities, but it does not
follow conversely that the production of commodities is a necessary
condition for the division of labor. In the primitive Indian community there is a social division of labor, without production of com-

modities."[46] In communism, as in a primitive Indian community, labor is not a commodity, and commodities are not produced by labor.

Just as division of labor is historically characteristic of all economies, so is surplus-labor. The important point is the form that surplus-value takes under the commodity mode of production as opposed to non-commodity modes of production. Under a non-commodity mode of production, such as feudalism, surplus-value takes the form of use-value for the exploiter and does not result in the generation of "boundless thirst" for further surplus-value.[47] In the commodity mode of production, the suffering of the exploited becomes unbearable because surplus-value takes the form of exchange-value, i.e., it is sold for money on the market and accumulated in the form of money or capital. The importance of the different form given to surplus-value under the commodity as opposed to a non-commodity mode of production is especially emphasized by Marx when he writes:

> It is, however, clear that in any given economic formation of society, where not the exchange value but the use-value of the product predominates, surplus-labor will be limited by a given set of wants which may be greater or less, and that here no boundless thirst for surplus-labor arises from the nature of production itself. Hence in antiquity overwork becomes horrible only when the object is to obtain exchange value in its specific independent money-form; in the production of gold and silver.[48]

The unique characteristic of the commodity mode of production, i.e., the separation between producer and user bridged only by the "cash nexus," is the source of all the specific economic ills, such as crises, and the alienation of man, attributed by Marx to capitalism. According to Marx, capitalist society is destined to be destroyed by the inherent contradictions that result from commodity production, and in the socialist society that arises commodities are not to be produced. Instead, society distributes its labor and means of production in accordance with a consciously formulated social plan. This is the reason for the efforts toward centralized allocation of supply in the

46. Marx, *Capital*, vol. I (Modern Library), p. 49.
47. Under communism, surplus-value takes the form of use-value for the community.
48. Marx, *Capital*, vol. I (Modern Library), p. 260.

Soviet Union. Production within the state sector for the state sector must not have the appearance of commodity production.[49]

49. It is not necessary to argue that economic decisions in the Soviet Union are still discussed and made in the original Marxian terms. It is true that Marxian views concerning commodity production have been rejected (or forgotten) by many "rationalized" Soviet economists. It is also true that the only part of the ideological program that has been achieved in the Soviet Union is the absence of private property in industrial production; and, therefore, modern Soviet ideologists might not subscribe to Marx's views but focus instead on property relations as the essential distinction between capitalism and socialism. These facts, however, are not damaging to the argument. People everywhere live in institutions bequeathed to them by founders whose views they might reject. The Soviet Union lives with the institution of material supply, bequeathed by a time when the vision was different. That the heritage of Marxian ideas concerning economic organization is not accepted by many Soviet economists is reflected in the fact that they no longer accept the institution that is a product of those ideas and are attempting to change it.

CHAPTER 2

"War Communism"—Product of Marxian Ideas

The effort today in the Soviet Union to avoid the appearance of commodity production in the state sector is a simulacrum of the high hopes and efforts of the first years of the revolution. This chapter documents these hopes and their frustration. To explain the economic history of war communism as a product of Marxian ideas challenges the prevalent interpretation of the economic policies of this period as temporary expedients to meet wartime and inflationary conditions. Although there are scholars whose accounts are notable exceptions to this interpretation, it is the dominant one and is found in popular and scholarly works, textbooks, and other sources. For example, Nettl states that war communism "represented a series of *ad hoc* measures to combat emergency situations."[1] Sherman writes that "as a necessary military measure, by the end of 1918 all large-scale factories had been nationalized and put under central control," and he explains the requisitioning and allocation in kind of supplies from farm and factory as the consequence of inflation having ended the usefulness of money.[2] Anderson states that with the outbreak of the civil war in May 1918 "an emergency policy of War Communism was adopted."[3] Fainsod states that "the policy of War Communism

1. J. P. Nettl, *The Soviet Achievement* (New York: Harcourt, Brace and World, 1967), p. 76.
2. Howard J. Sherman, *The Soviet Economy* (Boston: Little, Brown & Co., 1969), p. 59.
3. Thornton Anderson, *Russian Political Thought* (Ithaca, N.Y.: Cornell University Press, 1967), p. 322.

was the rule of the besieged fortress."[4] This chapter will show by a study of Lenin's writings during the war communism period that this prevalent interpretation suffers from the neglect of the original aspirations of Marxian socialism and consequently misrepresents the motives behind the economic policies of war communism.[5]

The Marxian foundation of war communism has not always been neglected.[6] During the 1920s and 1930s, Western students[7] of the war communism period, though they did not deny the impact of conditions of war and necessity, attempted to explain the economic policies of the period with regard to the Marxian aspirations. Although the Marxian motivation behind the program was not systematically explained, the economic program of war communism was seen as an effort to replace the kind of economic relationships that are found in the market economy with socialist non-market allocation of resources and distribution of products. The earlier accounts explained that the economic policies of war communism so disorganized production that its drastic decline forced an end to the

4. Merle Fainsod, How Russia Is Ruled (Cambridge, Mass.: Harvard University Press, rev. ed., 1963), p. 93.

5. The Marxian intentions and aspirations of the Bolshevik economic program were understood by only relatively few of the participants whose intellect permitted abstract thought and comprehension of general principles. Even many of the most fanatical never understood the revolution in terms beyond corrupted class-war terms, which were partially the result of efforts to communicate Marxian socialism to the masses. Perhaps large numbers of the revolutionary masses understood the revolution only in terms of personal gain through personal vengeance and permissible robbery of the upper classes. However this may be, the Marxian aspirations of the Bolsheviks constituted a comprehensive program of economic, political, and social destruction and reconstruction. A widespread state of "moral inversion" may have contributed fanaticism and ruthlessness on a scale necessary for Bolshevik success in achieving and maintaining power. For the analysis of "moral inversion," see Michael Polanyi, "Beyond Nihilism" in Knowing and Being: Essays by Michael Polanyi, edited by Marjorie Grene (Chicago: University of Chicago Press, 1969), pp. 3-23.

6. The neglect of Marxian aspirations is characteristic not only of studies of specific periods but of the general outlook. For example, Alexander Gerschenkron writes that "the Soviet government can be properly described as a product of the country's economic backwardness" (Economic Backwardness in Historical Perspective, Cambridge, Mass.: Harvard University Press, 1962, p. 28). Gerschenkron does not recognize Marxian doctrine as a significant force in Soviet history (see, for example, his Continuity in History and Other Essays, Cambridge, Mass.: Harvard University Press, 1968, pp. 69, 490).

7. See, for example, Arthur Z. Arnold, Banks, Credit, and Money in Soviet Russia (New York: Columbia University Press, 1937); Boris Brutzkus, Economic Planning in Soviet Russia (London: Routledge, 1935); Michael S. Farbman, Bolshevism in Retreat (London: Collins, 1923); Lancelot Lawton, An Economic History of Soviet Russia, 2 vols. (London: Macmillan, 1932); A. Yugoff, Economic Trends in Soviet Russia (New York: R. R. Smith, 1930).

attempt to establish socialism on the basis of the socialist ideas of that time. Some writers perhaps thought that the effort would have fared better if it had not been for the lack of control because of civil war. But others, such as Brutzkus[8] and Lawton,[9] pointed out that the economic system of war communism suffered from defects that would have doomed the system just as certainly under conditions of peace.[10]

The change of mind in the West since these earlier accounts has established an interpretation prevalent in Western scholarship that is remarkably close to the official party "line" of the Stalin era.[11] To account for this similarity is important. To suggest that numerous Western scholars consciously follow the line of the Stalin era would not be satisfactory. The prevalent interpretation of the policies of war communism as pragmatic, temporary expedients to meet wartime and inflationary conditions derives primarily from Western and not Soviet writers. It was Dobb's account, reinforced by that of Carr, that convinced numerous Western scholars. Therefore, the critical an-

8. Brutzkus, *Economic Planning in Soviet Russia*.
9. Lawton, *Economic History of Soviet Russia*.
10. Brutzkus reports that in keeping with the Marxian principle of a moneyless economy, the production of enterprises was put at the disposal of the *Glavki* without being brought to a common denominator. The *Glavki* had no basis for assessing outputs of enterprises and their relative productivities and thereby no rational basis for the allocation of factors of production. The effort to establish an economy *in natura*, or to organize it along the lines of a peasant community or a factory, broke down because the economic system of a peasant community and that of a socialist state are not comparable in size. "In such cases differences in degree become differences in kind"(*Economic Planning in Soviet Russia*, p. 37). Brutzkus notes that the attempt resulted in a lesson learned and that the Five Year Plan was founded on the basis of a money economy.
Lawton gives the same account of the breakdown. He writes that "one of the chief causes of industrial collapse was disregard of economic calculation. This disregard was as much the consequence of policy as of unavoidable circumstance" (*Economic History of Soviet Russia*, p. 107). Finding itself with no basis for making allocative-distributive decisions, the Supreme Economic Council retreated to preferential allocation to "essential" industries and experienced for the first time the problem of discriminating between the essential and the non-essential in an interdependent system.
In *The Logic of Liberty* (Chicago: University of Chicago Press, 1951), Michael Polanyi gives a more general theoretical statement as to why centralized planning as originally intended is impossible.
11. The official line of the Stalin era was a while in forming. There was a serious scholarly literature in Russia during the 1920s that was quite different. Although the official line on war communism is still followed in recent Soviet general works in which the interpretation of many issues is the product of politically guided editorial conferences, it is being gradually undermined in the Soviet Union by a new monographic literature in which various policies of the war communism period are studied.

alysis of this chapter is directed primarily at the accounts by Dobb and Carr. This book offers no analysis of the Soviet literature on war communism. Nevertheless, Lenin's testimony on the matter would seem to be a standard by which to judge any interpretation.

The Prevalent Interpretation

Dobb states that the system of war communism "emerges clearly as an empirical creation, not as the *a priori* product of theory: as an improvisation in face of economic scarcity and military urgency in conditions of exhausting civil war."[12] However, the documentation supplied by Dobb as evidence of his interpretation is weak. He dismisses the considerable evidence against his interpretation with his argument that statements of Bolsheviks and Soviet officials and in official decrees and resolutions *made during the period of war communism* were "no more than flights of leftist fancy."[13] Dobb relies on statements made by Lenin *after the event* and does not produce a single statement made during the war communism period that the policies were improvisations in response to the economic and military conditions. He produces no statements made at the time of the decrees and resolutions which indicate that the measures were considered to be temporary and would be removed with a return to peace.

The term "New Economic Policy" and Lenin's efforts to defend the policy as a socialist one imply that there was a previous socialist economic policy. Indeed, Lenin's polemics against the communist diehards for their dogmatism even in the face of disaster are non-sensical unless the policies of war communism were regarded as constituting a socialist program.

The weakness of Dobb's interpretation is sharply brought out by the way Davies presents the same interpretation. He writes that "the extension of the civil war from 1918 onwards resulted in a further rapid decline in industrial and agricultural production. The extreme measures of war communism were in essence emergency methods by which the government acquired a maximum share of this reduced

12. Maurice Dobb, *Soviet Economic Development Since 1917* (London: Routledge and Kegan Paul, Ltd., 1966), p. 122.
13. Ibid.

output and allocated it to what it regarded as the most essential uses."[14] He goes on to write that "there was a tendency to treat decisions arising out of war needs as matters of high principle" (p. 34). Davies takes this position in general and argues it specifically in regard to the resolutions passed in May 1919 by the Congress of Representatives of Financial Departments "calling for the fusion of local finance with general state finance, for all local financial expenditure to be made via the appropriate central commissariat" (pp. 33-34). Davies argues that "the real justification for this change in policy lay in the emergency conditions, which made drastic incursions into local spending powers inevitable" (p. 34).

But Davies himself points out that "it was not until the middle of 1920 that the division of budgets into state and local was formally abolished" (p. 34). This is a very long wait for implementing a resolution passed because of emergency conditions. Davies points out that by the time of implementation "the money budget had lost virtually all practical importance" (p. 35).

Thus, the account given by Davies does not seem to support his thesis. If the centralization of finance was regarded as a necessary war or anti-inflationary measure, someone would have said so and the measure would have been decided before it became meaningless as a tool of financial control over a year later. Davies never gives any explanation of why, if the measures were war or anti-inflationary, they were not discussed as such. Davies's position is that, in spite of the fact that those involved at the time regarded the matter as one of principle, the decision was determined by war necessity. This means that the terms in which the issue was fought and decided had no connection with the decision! It cannot be more completely denied that the ideas of men have any effect on their affairs.

In his interpretation of war communism, Carr provides a blend of the influences of ideology and wartime expediency.[15] However, his "blend" is mainly one of contradictory statements that acknowledge the ideological motivation of war communism and then attribute its policies to the conditions of the time. Even when he qualifies the interpretation of war communism as a response to conditions of war,

14. R. W. Davies, *The Development of the Soviet Budgetary System* (Cambridge: Cambridge University Press, 1958), p. 26.
15. E. H. Carr, *The Bolshevik Revolution, 1917-1923*, vol. II (New York: Macmillan, 1952).

it is in terms of prior conditions: "The civil war hastened the adoption throughout the whole field of economic policy of a series of measures which came to be known as 'war communism.' But the changes had to some extent been prepared by what went before; and nowhere was this more marked than in agrarian policy, where the threat of hunger had already begun to shape those forms of organization which the emergency of the civil war was to complete" (p. 53). Although Carr is able to state the original socialist program, in his account the socialist aspirations become ancillary, and ideological motivation is pushed into the background.

The result is to limit the role of ideology to that of producing rationales for objectively determined events. For example: "The argument for the permanent and unlimited conscription of labour by the state, like the contemporary argument for the abolition of money, reads like an attempt to provide a theoretical justification for a harsh necessity which it had been impossible to avoid" (p. 216). The march into socialism was not a product of conscious design based on theoretical principle although it may have *seemed* that way to the Bolsheviks: "The essence of the labor policy of war communism was the abandonment of the labor market and of recognized capitalist procedures for the engagement and management of the workers; and this made it seem, like other policies of the period, not merely a concession to the needs of the civil war, but an authentic advance into the socialist order" (p. 207). Although one can find evidence in Carr that contradicts his emphasis on the expedient character of the policies, the effect of his account, which acknowledges ideological motives and then subordinates this influence by giving a deterministic explanation of the practical necessity for the policies, is to reinforce the more simplistic account of Dobb.

Following Carr, it is often said that war communism was the product of theory and necessity, but even those who admit ideological motivation find it difficult to stress because they do not seem to understand the Marxian economic program. As a consequence they are forced to account for the policies in terms of the conditions of the time. For example, Daniels states that war communism was "an attempt by force and bureaucratic centralization to transform Russian society overnight into the communist ideal."[16] He then says that the

16. R. V. Daniels, *Russia* (Englewood Cliffs, N.J.: Prentice-Hall, 1964), p. 90.

requisitioning of food from the peasants "became necessary to feed
the army and the cities when the production of goods for sale to the
peasants broke down and money became worthless" (p. 91). Elsewhere he writes: "The most severe economic feature of War Communism was the requisitioning—in effect, confiscation—of food supplies from the peasantry. Such violent measures were required to forestall the urban starvation which was threatened by the breakdown of
normal trade."[17]

The principle of surplus appropriation was the crux of the socialist
program. Its purpose was to eliminate purchase and sale on the market and to replace private market exchange of goods between industry
and agriculture with socialist distribution of products in kind. It is
incongruous to recognize the ideological motivations of war communism and then explain the backbone of the ideological program
as a product of necessity and the conscious destruction of commercial
principles as a "breakdown of normal trade."

The effect of the civil war on the socialist policy was to reduce the
organizational principle of surplus appropriation to confiscation by
the "iron detachments." It was not the policy but the manner in
which it was applied that was determined by civil war. Furthermore,
the application of force was not simply the product of civil war. The
policies of the Bolsheviks had so disorganized industry that there
were no goods to be distributed to the peasants.

There are ideological interpretations of war communism in terms
that do not reflect the intentions of the economic program of
Marxian socialism. For example, Ulam interprets war communism as
policies designed by Lenin to win the workers over to Bolshevism.[18]
Although Ulam recognizes ideological motivation for war communism, he represents the policies as constituting a political, rather than
an economic, program intended to be temporary. Unable to give the
workers peace or enough bread, the Bolsheviks gave them the satisfaction of being the boss and of having the peasant stripped of his
surplus in order to feed the new boss. Once Lenin had the allegiance
of the workers, it was time "for the Communist Party to kill War
Communism" (p. 468).

17. R. V. Daniels, *The Conscience of the Revolution* (Cambridge, Mass.: Harvard
University Press, 1960), p. 94.
18. Adam Ulam, *The Bolsheviks* (New York: Macmillan, 1965), p. 467.

Such a political interpretation does not take into account two important facts: (1) Workers and peasants were not generally distinct classes. The workers were still closely connected with the agrarian population and were to a great extent an overflow of the land-starved peasantry. Familial connections between town and country were extensive, and during the period of war communism the return of workers to the land occurred on a large scale. (2) The policies of war communism were not generally popular with the workers. The strong influence of the meetings and strikes of the Petrograd workers on the Kronstadt sailors in February 1921 is known.[19] The Kronstadt rising was an expression of widespread conflict between the masses and the Bolshevik government. The workers were particularly irked by efforts of the regime to prevent individuals from provisioning themselves with necessities, but, as Katkov states, the widespread opposition to the political and economic policies of the Bolsheviks was one of fundamental principle: "The popular masses were beginning to understand that the ideal order towards which the leadership of the Communist Party was steering the Soviet State was based on a principle according to which all efforts of individual members of the community were to be regimented so as to serve exclusively the needs of society as a whole. What these needs were was to be determined by the Communist leadership of the State, which undertook, in exchange for their loyalty and total submission to the State and Party directives, to provide for all individual citizens those needs which the leadership considered legitimate. This Marxist ideal was fundamentally unacceptable not only to the peasantry, but also to a large part of the town proletariat" (p. 51).

The Evidence from Lenin

Whatever the validity of my analysis to this point, the interpretation of war communism as policies of expediency can be examined in the light of Lenin's writings, to which we now turn. Socialist planning, as understood by Lenin and as contrasted by him with capitalist planning, meant the replacement of commodity production with centralized production and non-market allocation and

19. See, for example, George Katkov, "The Kronstadt Rising," *St. Antony's Papers,* Number 6 (London: Chatte & Windus, 1959), pp. 11-74.

distribution. In place of production by autonomous producers for exchange on the market guided by commercial principles, there would be socially organized production for direct use by the community. The economic policies of war communism were a product of this Marxian framework.

Writing in August 1917 in *State and Revolution*, Lenin states that "to organize the *whole* national economy on the lines of the postal service . . . all under the control and leadership of the armed proletariat—this is our immediate aim. This is the state and this is the economic foundation that we need" (vol. 25, p. 427).[20]

In September 1917 in "The Impending Catastrophe and How to Combat It," Lenin attribtues the disorganization of the Russian economy to the lack of central control. He says that the need for central control "is indisputable and universally recognized" and that the needed measures "are *not* being adopted *only* because, exclusively because, their realization would affect the fabulous profits of a handful of landowners and capitalists" (vol. 25, p. 324). According to Lenin the measures needed for control are very simple and "people who counter us with the argument that socialism cannot be introduced are barefaced liars" because "the vast majority of commercial and industrial establishments are now working not for the 'free market,' but *for the government*" (p. 340). He depicts the Social Revolutionaries and Mensheviks as "scared Philistines" for arguing that Russia cannot get along without the capitalists who would run away if too severe measures were adopted (p. 342). He says that one cannot be a revolutionary if one fears to advance toward socialism and depicts the Social Revolutionaries and Mensheviks as "pseudo-Marxist lackeys of the bourgeoisie" for claiming that it is too early to establish socialism in Russia (pp. 356-57). He sees universal labor conscription as a "step towards the regulation of economic life as a whole in accordance with a certain general plan" (p. 359).

The "Draft Decree on the Nationalization of the Banks and on Measures Necessary for its Implementation" was written in the first half of December 1917, immediately after the Bolshevik seizure of

20. The quotations are cited from the 1960-68 English translation (London: Lawrence & Wishart) of the *Collected Works*. To avoid numerous footnotes, page and volume references are given in the text. It is not a purpose of this study to show the specific influence of others on Lenin's thought. It should not be assumed that all the ideas quoted from Lenin were original with him.

power. According to Dobb the nationalization of banks announced on December 17, 1917, "was primarily undertaken to counter a strike of civil servants and employees of the State Bank."[21] Although the implementation of the policy at that point in time may have been triggered by a strike, the policy itself was not a product of strike conditions. Item 5 of the Draft Decree states that "general labor conscription is introduced," and item 7 states that "for the purpose of proper accounting and distribution of food and other necessities, every citizen of the state shall be obliged to join a consumers society" (vol. 26, p. 392). It would seem that the nationalization of banks, rather than being a mere emergency response to forestall a strike, was viewed as a part of a more general economic program and that such ideas of economic organization were in Lenin's mind prior to the later events that are said to have evoked them.[22]

In the "Political Report of the Central Committee," delivered at the Seventh Party Congress on March 7, 1918, Lenin states that the bourgeois revolution differs from the socialist revolution in finding ready-made forms of capitalist relationships; "Soviet power does not inherit such ready-made relationships. . . . The organization of accounting, of the control of large enterprises, the transformation of the whole of the state economic mechanism into a single huge machine, into an economic organism that will work in such a way as to enable hundreds of millions of people to be guided by a single plan —such was the enormous organizational problem that rested on our shoulders" (vol. 27, pp. 90-91).

Lenin writes in "The Immediate Tasks of the Soviet Government," published in the April 28, 1918 issue of *Pravda*, that thanks to the peace the Russian Soviet Republic has an opportunity to concentrate efforts on the task of socialist organization (vol. 27, p. 237). This principal task is "the positive or constructive work of setting up an extremely intricate and delicate system of new organization rela-

21. Dobb, *Soviet Economic Development Since 1917*, pp. 83-84.

22. Carr reports that a resolution prepared by Lenin, approved by the Bolshevik central committee, and passed by a conference of representatives of factories and committees in Petrograd on May 30, 1917, "constituted the most important Bolshevik pronouncement before the revolution on the organization of industry." The resolution spoke of "the need of an 'all-state organization' for the purpose of 'the organization on a broad regional and finally all-state scale of the exchange of agricultural implements, clothing, boots and similar goods' for 'general labor service' " (*Bolshevik Revolution*, pp. 60-61).

tionships extending to the planned production and distribution of
the goods required for the existence of tens of millions of people"
(p. 241). He says that from October 1917 until March-April 1918
the resistance of the exploiters took the form of open civil war and
prevented socialist organization from being the main and central
task. However, once the Bolsheviks won Russia, socialist organization
was the main and central task. He says that

> for the first time in human history a socialist party has managed to com-
> plete in the main the conquest of power and the suppression of exploit-
> ers, and has managed to approach directly the task of administration.
> We must prove worthy executors of this most difficult (and most grat-
> ifying) task of the socialist revolution. We must fully realize that in
> order to administer successfully, besides being able to convince people,
> besides being able to win civil war, we must be able to do practical
> organizational work. This is the most difficult task, because it is a matter
> of organizing in a new way the most deep-rooted, the economic, founda-
> tions of life of scores of millions of people. And it is the most gratifying
> task because only after it has been fulfilled (in the principal and main
> outlines) will it be possible to say that Russia has become not only a
> Soviet, but also a Socialist Republic (pp. 242-43).

He goes on to say that "without comprehensive state accounting and
control of production and distribution of goods, the power of the
working people, the freedom of the working people, cannot maintain itself, and that a return to the yoke of capitalism is inevitable"
(pp. 253-54).

It might be objected that Lenin conceived of such statements only
as propaganda necessary to overshadow criticism of the Brest-Litovsk
Treaty or as a warning to go slow in the building of socialism. However that may be, neither objection is damaging to the point. That a
treaty so strongly opposed and denounced could be excused on the
grounds that it provided an opportunity for introducing socialism is
evidence of the importance placed on the introduction of socialism.
Similarly, to warn of the difficulties in introducing such a totally new
form of economic organization was pointless unless it was the intention to introduce socialism.

Moreover, to classify Lenin's statements as pure propaganda is
difficult. It is hard to read "The Immediate Tasks of the Soviet
Government" without feeling that Lenin is sincere in the importance

he places on socialist organization but that he has no clear idea how to achieve the organization of an economy that does not produce "commodities." He sometimes seems to hope that socialism will implement itself. It is a noticeable characteristic of some of the writing of the time that socialism was something so passionately willed that it was thought bound to occur.

In "Left-wing Childishness and Petty-bourgeois Mentality" in the May 9, 10, and 11, 1918 issues of *Pravda*, Lenin replies to the "left communists" and their charge of "state capitalism." He is obviously worried about succeeding in socialist organization and concerned about the consequent vulnerability of socialism in Russia. He maintains that the left communists in their "Theses on the Present Situation" are concerned with nationalizing and crushing the bourgeoisie and that these were the tasks of yesterday. "Today only a blind man could fail to see that we have nationalized, confiscated, beaten down and put down more *than we have been able to keep count.* The difference between socialization and simple confiscation is that confiscation can be carried out by 'determination' alone, without the ability to calculate and distribute properly, *whereas socialization cannot be brought about without this ability*" (vol. 27, p. 334). Lenin's criticism of the left communists is not a disagreement over the basic economic program,[23] and it is not a concession to the economic backwardness of Russia. Rather, he is critical of the left for not being realistic about the speed with which to proceed with the breakup of the existing economic organization. Perhaps a deeper realization was beginning also. Once Lenin was in power there was pressure, perhaps for the first time in his life, for his economic thinking to bear on reality. If Lenin began to recognize utopianism in the program of action called for by his Marxian heritage, it was the result of inability to organize socialistically what had been or-

23. No Marxian socialist thought that a system of commodity production was a socialist economy. This agreement on basic principle is sometimes obscured by the interpretation of the conflict between "anarchic" and "bureaucratic" preferences. The fight over "workers' control" was not a fight over planning, and when the planned regulation of the national economy by workers' control failed, it was workers' control and not planning that was abandoned. The leftist preference for planning by collegial administration was partially defeated by the practical problem of determining responsibility for action or inaction under such a system. Such practical faults of a hierarchy of collegia and the chaos of workers' control lent authority to Lenin's insistence on the necessity for individual authority.

ganized by the market relationships that had been destroyed. If Lenin became skeptical of further destruction of market relationships, it was because reality bore hard upon him.

As it dawned on Lenin that the expressed intentions that were the foundation of the revolution might themselves have no basis in reality, he found himself in a position that would have devoured others. When Lenin sensed that in spite of its passion and fierceness the revolution could not shape reality to its will, he faced the problem of leading a revolution whose practical intentions were impossible to achieve. His problem thereafter was to shape the economic doctrine and intentions to what could be achieved, while at the same time claiming the authority of the doctrine for this very purpose.[24] He covered every revision with personal vilification of critics and opponents. It is certain that Lenin did not have an explicit awareness of the problem he faced. The lucidity of an explicit formulation of the problem would have destroyed his faith.

Whatever the validity of my analysis of the situation in which Lenin found himself, it is clear from his writings that he regarded the policies of war communism as an effort to establish socialism. Whatever his opposition, if any, to the program during the period itself he does not refer to its policies as temporary or wartime measures.

On May 26, 1918 in a speech to the First Congress of Economic Councils, Lenin says that "things are not so simple in regard to the organization of the economy on socialist lines" (vol. 27, p. 409). Such a statement implies that there was an effort to so organize the economy. Lenin attributes the economic problems of the time to bourgeois saboteurs, to lack of socialist experience, and especially to bad labor discipline. He does not blame civil war.

In the economic section of "The Draft Program of the R.C.P.(B.)

24. Lenin might have regarded the reconciliation of socialism with commodity production as a temporary policy. He might have thought that NEP would extend over a period during which industrial production would be increased and a socialist consciousness instilled in the population. With more products available for distribution and socialist consciousness at a higher level, Lenin might have thought a second attempt to eliminate commodity production would be successful. However, the reconciliation Lenin began has developed to the point that today economic theorists cannot distinguish essential differences between models of socialist planning and models of commodity production. All pronouncements about the Soviet achievement overlook the failure of a revolution whose intention was to replace a system of commodity production with a system of socialist planning.

[Russian Communist Party—Bolshevik] Lenin writes that "in the sphere of distribution, the present task of the Soviet government is to continue steadily replacing trade by the planned, organized and nation-wide distribution of goods" (vol. 29, p. 137). He writes that "it is impossible to abolish money at one stroke in the first period of transition from capitalism to communism" but "the R.C.P. will strive as speedily as possible to introduce the most radical measures to pave the way for the abolition of money, first and foremost to replace it by savings books, checks, short-term notes entitling the holders to receive goods from the public stores, and so forth. . . . Practical experience in paving the way for, and carrying out, these and similar measures will show which of them are the most expedient" (pp. 137-38).

Writing in August 1919, Lenin says that "freedom to trade in grain is a return to capitalism" and that the whole trouble and danger is that large numbers of people, especially peasants, do not realize it (vol. 29, p. 570).

In his article, "Economics and Politics in the Era of the Dictatorship of the Proletariat," in the November 7, 1919 issue of *Pravda*, Lenin writes that although "state-organized distribution of products in place of private trade, i.e., the state procurement and delivery of grain to the cities and of industrial products to the countryside," has just begun and "peasant farming continues to be petty commodity production," improvement in the achievement of socialism in Russia is steady and "is being achieved in spite of the difficulties without world parallel, difficulties due to the Civil War organized by Russian and foreign capitalists" (vol. 30, pp. 109-10). The bourgeois world is raging against Bolshevism "because it realizes full well that our success in reconstructing the social economy is inevitable, provided we are not crushed by military force" (p. 110). He says that it is the conditions of commodity production that turn the peasant into a huckster and a profiteer (p. 113).

In the "Report on the Work of the All-Russian Central Executive Committee and the Council of People's Commissars to the First Session of the All-Russian Central Executive Committee of the 7th Convocation," February 2, 1920, Lenin says that a most important problem confronting them is that of "drawing the mass of people into administrative work" (vol. 30, p. 328). He criticizes leaders of co-

operatives who view cooperatives as "merely another form of capitalist economy and the notorious freedom of trade" (p. 329). Instead,
Lenin says, the Bolsheviks have set as a task and are working systematically to organize "the whole of the Soviet Republic" as "one great
co-operative of working people" (p. 329). Lenin says that this will be
achieved "perhaps in a few weeks, or in a few months."

Lenin writes that although the war is not yet finished "in the main
the problem of war has been solved" (p. 331). The "whole of the
Soviet state machine which is geared to war" must be switched to
the new course of peaceful economic construction (p. 332). He sees
this task as one of applying military methods to the organization of
the economy. In 1920 this is the solution he sees for the cold and
famine "brought by the end of winter" (p. 333).

He writes that grain has been collected "by socialist, not capitalist
methods, by compulsory delivery of grain by the peasants at fixed
prices, and not by selling on the free market—and this means we have
found the way. We are certain that it is the correct way and that it
will enable us to achieve results which will ensure tremendous economic construction" (p. 333). Lenin sees a continuation of this program along with labor conscription and labor armies as the solution
to the problem of securing far greater participation by the mass of the
workers in constructing socialism and as the correct socialist answer
to the specific problem of transition from capitalism to socialism
faced by the R.C.P. He does not say that this program is forced on
them by civil war or that it is viewed as temporary. To the contrary,
he says that the war problem is largely solved and, therefore, the
building of socialism can proceed more rapidly.

No doubt it was a program affected by conditions of the time, but
the program was the product of a heuristic process in Lenin's mind
as to how to establish socialism in Russia. As he emphasized, how to
fight within capitalist society and the non-commodity character of
socialist society had long been decided, but there were no specific
doctrinal instructions as to how to create the socialist economy. The
transitional problem had to be worked out in theory and in circumstances in which the R.C.P.(B.) found itself. The question of
whether the destroyed bourgeois economy could be replaced occurred
to Lenin only after its destruction was under way. The solution of
the left was simply to call for more destruction.

As Lenin grappled with the problem within socialist bounds, he first attached increasing importance to the belief that somehow workers' initiative would operate the economy socialistically but then became disillusioned with this belief. By March 15, 1920, after the "bourgeois economy" was largely destroyed, Lenin reached the conclusion that communism could only be built upon the rationality of the bourgeois economy. Remnants of bourgeois culture, science, and technology must be treasured. "They are bad remnants, it is true, but there are no others. Whoever dreams of a mythical communism should be driven from every business conference, and only those should be allowed to remain who know how to get things done with the remnants of capitalism" (vol. 30, p. 430). "Let us frankly admit our complete inability to conduct affairs, to be organizers and administrators" (p. 431). The power of the proletariat no longer lies in the construction of the socialist society but in political power over the bourgeois whose technical and managerial expertise runs the economy (p. 431).

Yet the great hope Lenin placed in the *subbotniks* (voluntary work) expressed in "A Great Beginning" (vol. 29, pp. 411-33) in July 1919 was still present in May 1920. He speaks of the *subbotniks* as "a new national (and later an international) system of economy of world-historic importance" and says that "only the most contemptible people who have irrevocably sold themselves to the capitalists can condemn the utilization of the great First of May festival for a mass-scale attempt to introduce communist labor" (vol. 31, p. 123). It seems that when he becomes disillusioned with the selfishness of workers and peasants, he places faith in military organization having the "enthusiasm of the Red Army" and when he becomes disillusioned with bureaucracy, he returns to the hope of the achievement of socialist organization by voluntary work.

Writing in "The Single Economic Plan" (vol. 32, pp. 137-45) in the February 22, 1921 issue of *Pravda*, Lenin ridicules Kritsman, Larin, and Milyutin for their "scholasticism" in writing that the entire economy should be organized according to a single plan, and he applies the "single plan" concept to the electrification program instead. It is not the idea of the single plan that Lenin attacks. Rather, he identifies socialist organization with what is possible and central planning with specific crash programs. By this time he has come to recognize that the idea of the whole economy organized by a single plan is utopian, and he is out of sympathy with those who continue to espouse the original socialist intention.

By March 15, 1921, in the "Report on the Substitution of a Tax in Kind for the Surplus-Appropriation System at the Tenth Congress of the R.C.P.(B.)," those who hold to the original aims of socialism are "dreamers" instrumental in starting a socialist revolution but negative when insisting that economic affairs be run according to their intellectual constructions. Concessions must be made to the psychology of the peasant, "a certain freedom of exchange" is needed, and commodities must be produced. *This fundamental change was not introduced on the grounds that the civil war was over.* The Bolsheviks did not give up their program because it was a temporary wartime expedient unsuitable for peacetime conditions but because the peasants no longer feared the return of the landowners and ceased to tolerate the Bolshevik program.

Lenin says that from talks with comrades about the preliminary draft on replacing surplus appropriation by a tax, it is clear that such a replacement will allow commodity production. He says that "all of us who have studied at least the elements of Marxism know that this exchange and freedom of trade" is the source of capitalist evils (vol. 32, p. 218). The question of how the Communist Party can recognize and accept commodity exchange is judged by Lenin to be a legitimate and inevitable question (p. 218). "Anyone who expects to get the answer at this Congress will be disappointed" (p. 218). He maintains that the question must be decided in principle and "we must muster . . . all our theoretical forces, all our practical experience, in order to see how it can be done" (pp. 218-19). Lenin seems to say that commodity production must be reconciled with socialism because commodity production is a necessity. Lenin does not know how it can work in practice, but he wishes to show that theoretically it is conceivable (p. 220). If *"surplus-appropriation" had been a temporary expedient to meet wartime conditions, it could have been abandoned easily just on these terms, and the embarrassing, difficult doctrinal acrobatics would not have been necessary.*

Lenin mentions "the vastness of our agricultural country with its poor transport system" and the necessity of wartime measures (p. 219). But the war conditions are not given by Lenin as the reason for the measures to eliminate commodity production, and neither the backwardness of peasant Russia nor the return of peace are given as the reasons for abandoning the measures. Rather, the backwardness of Russia and the war are reasons why "we are very much to blame for having gone too far, we overdid the nationalization of industry and trade," clamping down on commodity production more than necessary (p. 219). "In this respect we have made many outright mistakes, and it would be a great crime not to see this and not to realize that we have failed to keep within bounds, and have not known where to stop" (p. 219). "It is an unquestionable fact that we went further than was theoretically and politically necessary" (p. 220).

He says that to "allow free local exchange to an appreciable extent" will not destroy but strengthen the political power of the proletariat (p. 220). This suggests that Lenin thought that the reintroduction of market exchange was necessary to retain power and that he understood the practical need to sacrifice doctrine to power rather than the other way around.

Lenin writes that the resolution of the Ninth Party Congress on the cooperatives was "based entirely on the principle of surplus-grain appropriation" (p. 221). This principle must be annulled by the Tenth Congress because "the resolution of the Ninth Congress assumed that we would be advancing in a straight line" (p. 221). But they had not advanced in a straight line, and the Bolsheviks must profit from experience and act to uphold their political interests (p. 221). In place of the former program, Lenin asks the Tenth Congress to adopt a resolution which he says is necessarily vague: "Why necessarily? Because if we are to be absolutely definite, we must know exactly what we are going to do over the year ahead. Who knows that? No one" (p. 221).

It is clear that the program of eliminating commodity production was abandoned not because it was a wartime measure unsuited to peacetime but because it had caused economic disruption and dissatisfaction that were threats to the political power of the Bolsheviks. The problem was to adapt economic doctrine to reality in a way that would not threaten the Bolsheviks' political power. What such a socialism was to be like and how it was to be reconciled with original doctrine Lenin did not know. He did know that "basically the situation is this: we must satisfy the middle peasantry economically and go over to free exchange; otherwise it will be impossible—economically impossible—in view of the delay in the world revolution, to preserve the rule of the proletariat in Russia. We must clearly realize this and not be afraid to say it" (p. 225). To critics who are ridiculing this new program because of its capitalistic features, Lenin answers that the socialist program would have worked except for the civil war and the delay in world revolution. At any rate the country is exhausted and "what is needed now is an economic breathing spell" (p. 224). Surplus appropriation failed because the distribution of products to the peasants broke down.

It is clear that the measures of war communism were based on an application of Marxian doctrine, that the debates concerning them were in doctrinal terms, and that their abandonment presented Lenin with serious doctrinal difficulties. As a final defense of the replacement of surplus appropriation by a tax, Lenin says that although surplus appropriation had been necessary because "our need was extreme . . . theoretically speaking, state monopoly is not necessarily the best system from the viewpoint of the interests of socialism" (p. 226). For the first time he suggests that the way out is to regard the abandoned socialist measures not as a mistake, as he had previously been saying, but as a necessity of the time.[25]

The erroneous interpretation of war communism as temporary measures to cope with war and inflation was founded on a fabrication and was recognized as such by Lenin. If the principle of surplus appropriation had been adopted as a temporary expedient to meet conditions of war and inflation, its abandonment would not have presented doctrinal difficulties. It is clear from the "Report on the Substitution of a Tax for the Surplus Appropriation System" that Lenin thought that abandonment of surplus appropriation presented doctrinal difficulties. He differed from dogmatists in realizing the necessity for the abandonment and the need to stretch doctrine to fit reality.

25. At the Eleventh Party Congress (vol. 33) as a defense against universal ridicule, Lenin says that the Bolsheviks have not failed because the decrees and resolutions of war communism were only intended as propaganda to convey to the masses the Bolshevik economic and political program. He does not disclaim the ideas behind the decrees and resolutions but disclaims only that the Bolsheviks ever intended to implement them. Simultaneously, he claims the measures were implemented because of war conditions.

In "The Fourth Anniversary of the October Revolution," *Pravda*, October 18, 1921, Lenin writes that it is in building the new socialist edifice "that we have sustained the greatest number of reverses and have made most mistakes" (vol. 33, p. 57). He goes on to say that the New Economy Policy (NEP) is "correcting a number of our mistakes." He reports that socialism is learning flexibility, i.e., the abandonment of paths that prove "to be inexpedient or impossible" (p. 58). He admits that "borne along on the crest of the wave of enthusiasm . . . we expected to accomplish economic tasks just as great as the political and military tasks" (p. 58). "We expected—or perhaps it would be truer to say that we presumed without having given it adequate consideration—to be able to organize the state production and the state distribution of products on communist lines in a small-peasant country directly as ordered by the proletarian state. Experience has proved that we were wrong" (p. 58).

Those who maintain that the policies of war communism were temporary measures to cope with war and inflation rather than an effort to establish socialist organization should explain why Lenin repeatedly described the policies as efforts to establish socialism. If they were wartime policies, why should Lenin not have said so? If in fact the measures were meant to be temporary and were a response to war and inflation, Lenin's admission that he and the R.C.P.(B.) had made mistakes in their efforts to introduce socialism was not only a needless and erroneous admission but also a fabrication. What purpose could have been served by such a fabrication? Such a blatant admission of the fallibility of the party could only have been a slip of honesty.

In November 1921, Lenin, still worried about criticism, asks in "The Importance of Gold" "how can we explain the transition from a series of extremely revolutionary actions to extremely 'reformist' actions in the same field at a time when the revolution as a whole is making victorious progress? Does this not imply a 'surrender of positions,' an 'admission of defeat,' or something of that sort?" (vol. 33, p. 109). If the policies of war communism had been viewed as temporary measures, it is difficult to see how such questions could have arisen and why Lenin thinks he must give a justification in doctrinal terms. He says explicitly that "we followed for more than three years, up to the spring of 1921 . . . a revolutionary approach to the problem—to break up the social-economic system completely at one stroke and to substitute a new one for it" (p. 110). Lenin says that since the spring of 1921, they have been adopting "a reformist type of method" (though we "have not yet fully realized it") in order "to *revive* trade, petty proprietorship, capitalism" (p. 110). He says that "compared with the previous, revolutionary approach, it is a reformist approach. . . . The question that arises is this. If, after trying revolutionary methods, you find they have failed and adopt reformist methods, does it not prove that you are declaring the revolution to have been a mistake in general?" (p. 110).

It is inconceivable that Lenin could have raised such a question if the measures of war communism were regarded as temporary expedients. Lenin's answer to his question is also inconceivable if the measures were temporary expedients:

> The greatest, perhaps the only danger to the genuine revolutionary is that of exaggerated revolutionism, ignoring the limits and conditions in which revolutionary methods are appropriate and can be successfully employed. True revolutionaries have mostly come a cropper when they began to write 'revolution' with a capital R, to elevate 'revolution' to something almost divine, to lose their heads, to lose the ability to reflect, weigh and ascertain in the coolest and most dispassionate manner at what moment, under what circumstances and in which sphere of action you must act in a revolutionary manner, and at what moment, under what circumstances and in which sphere you must turn to reformist action. True revolutionaries will perish (not that they will be defeated from outside, but that their work will suffer internal collapse) only if they abandon their sober outlook and take it into their heads that the 'great, victorious, world' revolution can and must solve all problems in a revolutionary manner under all circumstances and in all spheres of action. If they do this, their doom is certain (p. 111).

Lenin could have made his point in fewer words, but the point is clear: if socialist revolutionaries do not learn from the disasters that resulted from their attempts to organize a socialist economy and insist on maintaining and intensifying these measures, they will destroy themselves. It is not relevant whether the measures adopted were the best to achieve the original socialist aspirations or whether in the chaos of the period the measures were systematically applied to the economy. What is established is that (1) these measures were consistent with the expressed intentions and aspirations of scientific socialism, (2) they were considered at the time of their application to be steps in the building of socialist economy, (3) on the basis of results that Lenin attributed to the measures, he argued that they must be abandoned, and (4) he argued their abandonment in doctrinal terms that were not only difficult for him but would also have been beside the point and inconceivable if the measures of war communism were viewed as temporary, wartime expedients by the people who debated, passed, and implemented them.

Speaking on "Five Years of the Russian Revolution" delivered at the Fourth Congress of the Communist International on November 13, 1922, Lenin refers back to 1918 as "a time when we were more foolish than we are now" and "were every day hastily—perhaps too hastily—adopting various new economic measures which could not be described as anything but socialist measures" (vol. 33, p. 419). He says that he does not want to suggest that his first warnings about the socialist measures were made on the basis of "a ready-made plan of retreat" (p. 420). He says that his warnings made no mention of the very important need for free trade, but "they did contain a general, even if indefinite, idea of retreat" (p. 420). Lenin says that this "very vague idea" which he had as early as 1918 became very concrete in 1921 when "we felt the impact of a grave—I think it was the gravest—internal political crisis in Soviet Russia. This internal crisis brought to light discontent not only among a considerable section of the peasantry but also among the workers" (p. 421). Lenin asks what caused this "very unpleasant situation" and answers, "The reason for it was that in our economic offensive we had run too far ahead, that we had not provided ourselves with adequate resources, that the masses sensed what we ourselves were not then able to formulate consciously but what we admitted soon after, a few weeks later, namely, that the direct transition to purely socialist forms, to purely socialist distribution, was beyond our available strength, and that if we were unable to effect a retreat so as to confine ourselves to easier tasks, we would face disaster" (pp. 421-22).

How the Truth was Buried

In view of the evidence supplied by Lenin, corroborated by statements of Stalin,[26] Trotsky,[27] and numerous major and minor participants[28] in the effort to eliminate commodity production and construct an economic system organized by socialist principles, it is difficult to see why Dobb's interpretation gained such widespread acceptance. Part of the reason may be that there was occurring in the West a general shift in sympathy toward the Soviet Union's claim to be constructing a new kind of socio-economic system.[29]

26. Speaking on November 7, 1920, Stalin looks back on "Three Years of Proletarian Dictatorship" and says that "our work of construction during these three years has, of course, not been as successful as we would have liked to see it, but . . . in the first place, we had to build under fire. . . . Second, we were building not bourgeois economy, where everyone pursues his own private interests and does not worry about the state as a whole, pays no heed to the question of planned, organized economy on a national scale. No, we were building socialist society. This means that the needs of society as a whole have to be taken into consideration, that economy has to be organized on an all-Russian scale in a planned, conscious manner. No doubt this task is incomparably more complicated and more difficult" (The October Revolution, London: Martin Lawrence, 1934), p. 43.

27. See The Basic Writings of Trotsky, edited by Irving Howe (London: Secker & Warburg, 1963). Trotsky writes that "the period of so-called 'war communism' (1918-1921)" was a period when "economic life was wholly subjected to the needs of the front" (p. 160). Nevertheless, writes Trotsky, "it is necessary to acknowledge, however, that in its original conception it pursued broader aims. The Soviet government hoped and strove to develop these methods of regimentation directly into a system of planned economy in distribution as well as production. In other words, from 'war communism' it hoped gradually, but without destroying the system to arrive at genuine communism" (p. 161). He goes on to say that "reality, however, came into increasing conflict with the program of 'war communism.' Production continually declined, and not only because of the destructive action of the war" (p. 161). A result was that "the collapse of the productive forces surpassed anything of the kind that history had ever seen. The country, and the government with it, were at the very edge of the abyss" (p. 161). Trotsky then speaks of "the utopian hopes of the epoch of war communism" (p. 161), and says that even if revolution had occurred in the West, it can be said with certainty that "it would still have been necessary to renounce the direct state distribution of products in favour of the methods of commerce" (p. 162).

28. Victor Serge, in Memoirs of a Revolutionary (New York: Oxford University Press, 1963), writes that "the social system in these years was later called 'War Communism.' At the time it was called simply 'Communism,' and any one who, like myself, went so far as to consider it purely temporary was looked upon with disdain. Trotsky had just written that this system would last over several decades if the transition to a genuine, unfettered Socialism was to be assured. Bukharin . . . considered the present mode of organization to be final" (p. 115).

29. Interpretation of war communism as policies necessitated by the times was reinforced by methodologies whose accounts give no scope to ideas as autonomous forces in history—for example, deterministic accounts in which events are historically justified.

Among those whose methodologies do not preclude an ideological perspective, some have argued that the Bolsheviks could not have intended to implement socialism because

There is evidence for this hypothesis which can, perhaps, be considered now that great hopes for humanity are no longer placed on the outcome of Soviet socialism. The massacres of the First World War destroyed hopes and ideas along with lives. Many intellectuals abandoned belief in the inevitable progress of Western civilization. Some lost all hope; others placed their hopes for humanity on the Soviet Union, which claimed a new form of social system embodying human progress. The Great Depression resulted in a more general shattering of hopes and produced overnight from all classes of people radical criticism of market economy.[30] The general milieu affected reviews of accounts of Soviet experience.

For example, Lawton's two-volume work was reviewed by Eugene M. Kayden in the September 1933 issue of the *American Economic Review*. Kayden criticized Lawton for giving "recitals of Bolshevik horrors" and for having "nothing to say about social legislation and the education of labor," implying that Lawton's work was anti-Bolshevik propaganda and thereby unobjective and unscholarly. Lawton's account of the socialist program, the disastrous consequences, the abandonment of the program, and the evolution of a system (NEP) that the Bolsheviks could not define, was explained away by Kayden, who said that it was "too soon to judge of planned

Russia had not yet gone through the stage of bourgeois economy. To be consistent, those who make such an argument must also maintain that the Bolsheviks' actions did not constitute a socialist seizure of power because a genuinely proletarian class had not yet emerged.

Other writers have reformulated the intentions of the revolution such that they are made equivalent to its results. Such a methodology will always attribute success to the revolution. An example of this is the economists' interpretation of Soviet "planning." Since the outcome of Soviet planning has not been the elimination of commodity production but industrialization, writers state that the purpose of central planning was to achieve rapid industrialization. Such writers then account for the abandonment of central planning in the Soviet Union on the grounds that it has achieved its purpose. For example, H. S. Levine writes that "centralized planning has accomplished what its use was intended to accomplish: the radical and rapid structural transformation of the Soviet economy" ("Pressure and Planning in the Soviet Economy" in *Industrialization in Two Systems*, edited by Henry Rosovsky, New York: Wiley, 1966, p. 283). Besides obscuring the real reasons for which the efforts at planning are being abandoned, such accounts turn the Russian Revolution into a mere industrial revolution.

30. The views that blame market economy for being the cause of the Great Depression have influenced history for three decades. Even if policies resulting from such an interpretation of the depression have been beneficial, such an interpretation itself is questionable in view of the evidence that an erroneous policy of the Federal Reserve System, an agency of the United States government, was instrumental in placing the American economy in depression.

economy as a method of orderly economic development" and "premature to hold that in Bolshevik hands planning" is not capable of controlling and coordinating the whole economic life of the country. At a time when great hopes were placed on socialist planning, many did not want to hear of any failure.

In a review in the September 1935 issue of *The Economic Journal*, Maurice Dobb summarily dismissed Brutzkus on no other grounds than that "the author has had no direct contact with his country for the last decade."

Barbara Wootton reviewed Brutzkus in the August 1935 issue of *Economica*. She admitted that he relied wholly on documentary evidence in his account of the results of planning in the Soviet Union, but she suggested that his former "imprisonment and exile" had made his work unreliable and expressed her belief that "the author's own grievous sufferings" have at some points "distorted his view and undermined his regard for precision of statement." She did not, however, produce a single bit of evidence for her serious charge.

Wootton's irresponsible review can be understood by acknowledging her own hopes for planning, and the general breakdown in scholarly objectivity can be understood in terms of the widespread view of the time that capitalism and market economy had performed their historic functions and were destined to give way in the face of a superior socialist economy whose planning would prevent such things as the Great Depression. This view, which has proved to be absurd, was responsible for the frequent disregard of realities and the coloring of much scholarship. It was the Webbs's books that were influential, while those who did not abide by the definition of objective as that which is favorable to the Soviet Union were destined to be ignored.[31]

My account of the milieu of the time might seem controversial to some. Therefore, I let Paul T. Homan's article, "Economic Planning: the Proposals and the Literature," in the November 1932 issue of the *Quarterly Journal of Economics* recall the period. Homan surveys a large literature calling for planning in the United States

31. A copy of Farbman's book, *Bolshevism in Retreat*, that has been in the Bodleian Library at Oxford University since 1923, was read for the first time in November 1968, when I separated the uncut pages. Farbman, who had been in Russia during the war communism period as a correspondent of the *Manchester Guardian*, *The Observer*, and the *Chicago Daily News*, was an obvious source of information.

and notes that no one defines planning or explains how it is to function. No substantive meaning is given to central coordination but many attempt to win adherents to the idea of its necessity by accounts of the crises and evils of capitalism. He finds that even the economically literate writers about economic planning "are mostly persons to whom the theory of prices is distasteful, being by some strange process associated in their minds with a defense of laissez-faire." The numerous writers examined by Homan have a less definite idea of what this planning is that they are calling for than the Bolsheviks had fifteen years previously. This suggests that the power of the idea of planning evoked a general response unrelated to the socio-economic conditions of Russia and that its attraction was not lessened by the lack of a blueprint of how it would function. For those opposed to commodity production and for those who simply feared it, there had to be an alternative. The passion for planning launched books in the West that had no more foundation in reality than the program of action launched in Russia in 1917.

If we add to this milieu the fact that Western economists have never understood the economic intentions of Marxian socialism and even today can think of economic systems only in terms of optimality properties such as marginal conditions for economic efficiency, we can understand how even the most objective scholar might fail to establish the truth about war communism even for himself. The modern rationale for central planning—that it achieves rapid industrialization—is not the original Marxian rationale and formed after the original Marxian program was frustrated by a refractory reality. As has been seen, Lenin had sufficient intellectual honesty to realize that the Marxian program for the economy had been frustrated, and in 1921 he asked whether this meant that the revolution had been a mistake. However, not even Lenin had sufficient strength to answer in the affirmative; and so, out of the ruins of the original Marxian program emerged a new rationale for socialist planning. By the time of Dobb's writing, the original intentions of Marxian socialism had been pushed into the background, and it was neither in Stalin's interest nor in the interest of the myth of the infallibility of the party for Stalin to have encouraged the documentation by Soviet scholars of the war communism failure. If these original intentions are neglected, Dobb's account can seem plausible.

Although earlier Western interpretations stated unequivocally that it had been the intention during the war communism period to establish socialist planning, the Marxian motivation behind central planning was not adequately explained or related to the war communism policies. This inadequacy of the earlier accounts reduced their power to convince because in these accounts the Bolsheviks' economic policies seemed merely silly and irrational to Western scholars unfamiliar with the utopian character of the Marxian aspirations behind the policies. This weakness of the earlier accounts made it easier for them to be interpreted as anti-communist propaganda, whereas Dobb's account of the policies gave war communism a certain rationality due to necessity and, thus, gained ground as an objective account of the policies of war communism. This chapter does not pronounce on the objectivity of Dobb's interpretation but assesses its validity in the light of Lenin's testimony.

The association of socialist planning with doctrines of rapid industrialization has blinded scholars to the fundamental purpose of socialist economic organization. Its purpose was to eliminate commodity production and institute production for direct use by the socialist community. Even in 1952 we find this Marxian principle asserting itself through Stalin. In *Economic Problems of Socialism in the U.S.S.R.* (New York: International Publishers), he states that the output of the collective farms belongs to the farms and the state is in the role of outside customer. Therefore, the collective farm output

> goes into the market and is thus included in the system of commodity circulation. It is precisely this circumstance which now prevents the elevation of collective-farm property to the level of public property. It is therefore precisely from this end that the work of elevating collective-farm property to the level of public property must be tackled (p. 70).

Stalin's solution is that "collective-farm output must be excluded from the system of commodity circulation and included in the system of products-exchange between state industry and the collective farms" (p. 70). He says that direct exchange between town and country would have

> to be introduced without any particular hurry and only as the products of the town multiply. But it must be introduced unswervingly and un-

hesitatingly, step by step contracting the sphere of operation of commodity circulation and widening the sphere of operation of products-exchange.

Such a system, by contracting the sphere of operation of commodity circulation, will facilitate the transition from socialism to communism. Moreover, it will make it possible to include the basic property of the collective farms, the product of collective farming, in the general system of national planning (p. 70).

We find even for Stalin and as late as 1952 that the economic organization the Bolsheviks attempted to achieve in the war communism period remains the model for the communist economy. The frustration and economic irrationality that have resulted from efforts to establish a non-commodity mode of production in the Soviet Union have gradually eroded the Marxian aspiration. This aspiration and its effect on the operation of the Soviet economy have been obscured by the parochialism of Western economists who can envisage economic systems only in terms of growth rates, property rights, and optimality conditions for economic efficiency.

CHAPTER 3

Polycentricity and Hierarchy

Economists have sought to comprehend both the market economy and the Soviet economy in terms of their theoretical apparatus and have failed. Robert Campbell has expressed this failure as follows: "it may be that the conceptual dictionary of the economist is sufficiently circumscribed that he cannot compose an effective exposition of administrative economics relying on it alone."[1] He concludes that "it is probably necessary to go outside the language of economics to develop a generally useful theory of the administrative economy."[2] This chapter attempts to add to the conceptual dictionary of the economist and to outline a theoretical framework within which both the Soviet and market economies can be comprehended. It also shows the nature of hierarchy, the organizing power of which, unlike that of polycentricity, is limited by a span of control. In Chapter 4 the Soviet economy is interpreted in terms of polycentric organizational principles.

Traditionally, economic analysis has been circumscribed by the economist's concern with optimal resource allocation. This concern originates in the economist's definition of a market system as a price system. By thus defining an organizational system in terms of the signals upon which it relies, economists have restricted artificially their understanding of the generality of market processes. In this chapter the market system is treated as a member of the class of polycentric organizational systems and is defined in terms of organiza-

1. Robert Campbell, "On the Theory of Economic Administration" in *Industrialization in Two Systems*, edited by Henry Rosovsky (New York: Wiley, 1966), p. 202.
2. Ibid., p. 203.

tional principles general to polycentric systems.[3] The analysis in this chapter differentiates between the natural structure of the market system and the rules and signals used to condition its performance and thus offers the economist a more general conceptual framework.

An Organizational Model of the Market

When organization is achieved among people by their mutual interaction and initiative, the result is a system of mutual interdependence that cannot be subdivided into consecutive stages. Such a system is termed "polycentric" because all members in the interlocking and overlapping network of organization are free to undertake autonomous action that will bear on the actions of other members. Each member's autonomously chosen task comprises a part of the overall outcome and contributes toward its achievement. The result produced by the system is meaningful even though it is *ex ante* indeterminate. That is, although the outcome can be predicted, it is not predetermined but historically observable. The organization of science, democratic politics, and economic activity in a market system are characterized by polycentrism.

Diagrammatically, the organizational structure of a market system can be illustrated as in Figure 2. Each individual firm (a, b, c, d, e, f) has a hierarchic organizational structure, and each firm is interrelated to each of the others through the polycentric structure of the polygon. In Figure 2 each member, m, has $m - 1$ interrelations. There are two interrelations between two members, i.e., a adjusts to b and b adjusts to a. The total number of interrelations $R = m(m - 1)$.[4]

Imagine the expansion of Figure 2 by the addition of polygons (Figure 3).[5] In Figure 3, a, for example, has direct interrelations with members of three joining polygons, is indirectly interrelated to x through n and m, and is interrelated to y through, for example, an

3. Michael Polanyi introduced the concept of polycentricity into the study of scientific and economic organization. Polanyi's ideas have far-reaching implications and are difficult to summarize. For examples of his applications of principles of polycentricity, see *The Logic of Liberty* (Chicago: University of Chicago Press, 1951); and "The Republic of Science," *Minerva*, vol. 1 (October 1962), pp. 54-73.

4. I mean *inter*-relation in the sense that the lines (connections) between members of the polygon are dual. Alternatively, the total number of relations $R' = \dfrac{m(m-1)}{2}$.

5. The use of a uniform hexagon is arbitrary.

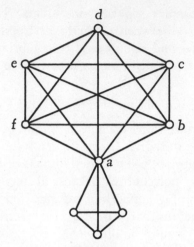

FIGURE 2.

indirect interrelation with x. Thus, a's autonomous actions will not equally affect all members of the polycentric organization. In the example, a's autonomous actions will bear more on b, c, d, e, f, g, h, i, j, k, m, n, and less on y.

Some of the direct and indirect interrelations may be "empty," and some of the interrelations may not be characterized by duality—for example, a's actions may affect b's actions, but b's actions may not affect a's actions. In this case b's interrelation to a is "empty," but a's

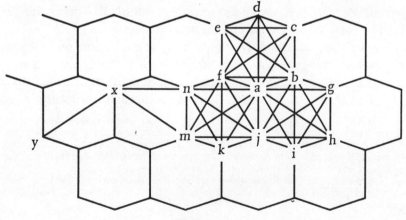

FIGURE 3.

interrelation to b is not. In this sense the interrelation between a and b degenerates into a relation in which b is sensitive to the autonomy of a, but a is not (perceptibly) sensitive to b.

Imagine the expansion of Figure 3 into a sphere. Imagine spheres inside interconnected spheres, and the organizational meaning of "periphery" and "center" firms becomes clear.[6] Center firms such as General Motors, whose autonomous actions have more impact on the economy, are located on the center sphere. The more numerous peripheral firms, such as a local construction company, are located on the outer sphere.

The greater autonomy and influence of an individual center firm, as contrasted with a peripheral firm, is reflected in the center firm having fewer empty interrelations and more interrelations in which duality is not present, i.e., more interrelations in which its autonomy affects other firms but is not (perceptibly) affected by that of other single firms.

The actions of members of a polycentric organization are said to be autonomous or free because they are not determined by instructions from a central superior. However, there are many ways in which the autonomy of members is restricted. The factors that condition the autonomy of firms in a market can be classified under three headings: the autonomy-limiting property inherent in polycentric organization, market criteria, and non-market criteria. Each, in turn, will be briefly outlined.

Autonomy-limiting Property of Polycentrism: The initiative taken by each member is limited by that taken by every other. Thus, the adjustment of each in respect to every other is related to the adjustment of everyone to each of the others. Such is the structure of mutual interdependence. Generally the initiative of everyone is not equal but depends on relative abilities, inheritances, motivations, political and social connections, personalities, etc.

Market Criteria: The governing functions of price and profit movements are established in economic theory; these are signals arising from the interaction of preferences within a polycentric organizational framework that add *economic efficiency* (in terms of consumer satisfaction) to the *organizational rationality* of the system. By

6. See Robert T. Averitt, *The Dual Economy* (New York: Norton, 1968), for the concepts of periphery and center firms.

referring to market signals generated by a process of mutual interaction, the director of each firm finds criteria, which his firm helps to determine, that aid him in deciding on his directives to subordinates. By continual reference and readjustment to the values generated in the market, each firm implements its own chosen task through continual recoordination of its efforts. In the absence of the price and profit signals, each director has no basis on which to judge if the summation of actions carried on within his firm comprises a meaningful, useful, or productive task. Herein lies a profound limitation to the firm: it cannot, on its own, determine all the criteria in the set of criteria to which it must adjust; it is simply one element of many influencing formation of these criteria.

Non-market Criteria: Non-market criteria emanate from government and tradition and subject the performance of a market economy to politics and social mores. They circumscribe producer and consumer preferences. Therefore, the performance of a market system is not independent of the rules, and the rules may be the source of social costs. Non-market criteria may be classed as follows:

(1) The autonomy of members is conditioned by the system of property rights and the rules governing the relationship between managers and owners.

(2) The actions of all members are circumscribed by the formal rules of the system. Such rules are impersonal and of uniform application and fall into two classes: (a) systems of rules, like that of contractual law, which apply to all participants irrespective of the specific kind of economic activity in which they are engaged; and (b) rules, such as those resulting from the Food and Drug Act, which apply to specific types of producers.

(3) The application of discretionary public authority will also condition the autonomy of members.

(4) Personal biases of some members may limit further the initiatives of other members, and the customs, mores, and traditions of the system will limit the success of the most creative and imaginative members, whether they be scientific and philosophical geniuses restricted by the authority of existing conceptual frameworks, or architects, artists, and writers who are "ahead of their time" (ahead of consumer tastes). Obviously, there is an interconnection between the informal rules of the system and the formal rules.

At any point in time the non-market criteria may be biased in favor of, or against, certain classes of individuals within a polycentric system, thus allowing some to take irresponsible prerogatives or denying others a greater realization of their abilities. The non-market criteria may be designed, or unintendedly serve, to allow privilege to a traditional oligarchy, enabling it to exert more initiative in the system than others. Or the criteria may foster equality of opportunity, so that those best endowed by nature to perform tasks assigned high marginal values have more influence within the system than others and become a natural oligarchy for the limited period of their successful lives. Or they may be egalitarian and frustrate abilities that are naturally superior in the same sense. Therefore, at any point in time, to the eyes of reformers the non-market criteria governing the system may appear to bear more heavily on some and less heavily on others.

The analysis in this section suggests an optimality property more general than the economist's traditional concern.[7] Figure 5 postulates

7. James M. Buchanan emphasizes the extension of the Pareto classification to organizational rules in "The Relevance of Pareto Optimality," *The Journal of Conflict Resolution*, vol. 6, no. 4 (December 1962), pp. 341-54.

As compared with my model (Figure 5), Figure 4 illustrates a model that seems implicit in Buchanan. Given an optimal set of rules, S_0, an optimal utility curve, U_0, is generated for given levels of resources (technology held constant). A non-optimal set of rules, S_1, generates less utility out of the same resources.

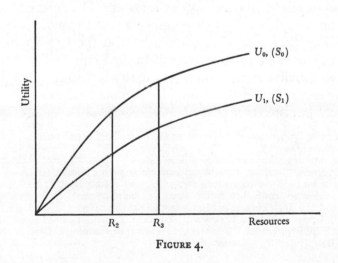

FIGURE 4.

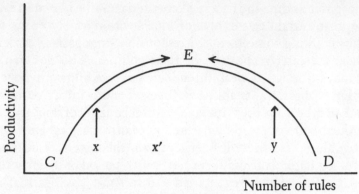

FIGURE 5.

the relationship between the number of rules governing the managers' choice and use of production functions and the productivity of the overall system.[8] Over a range, as the number of rules governing the productive behavior of managers increases, the overall productivity of the system increases. Beyond a certain point the productivity decreases. The reasons for this relationship are often recognized. The statement that laissez-faire could not exist in a pure form because the market system could not function without contractual law is recognition of the factors behind the upward sloping portion of the curve, and perhaps the Food and Drug Act, for example, by increasing consumer confidence in mass-produced processed foods and drugs, contributes to increased productivity of the system. The downward sloping portion is explained by the recognition that the more rules, the more stifling the manager's environment and the less his creative activity, the more of his time is spent in "red tape" rather than in productive activity; and, as the Hungarian economist Tibor Liska notes, the more contradictory the rules become,[9] eventually producing outputs unrelated to needs.

8. I am using "productivity" in the sense of "utility" or "social welfare." I do not mean gross physical output.
9. "The intricacy of economic life follows primarily from the fact that hosts of contrary tendencies must be brought into harmony with optimum efficiency. The stricter and more rigid the regulations prescribing the enforcement of such contrary tendencies, the more contradictory the directives must become. One receiving the directives has but a single choice: *not to observe all the directives*" ("The Development of Market Relations and of the Theory and Practice of Price Mechanism in Socialism," Lecture at CESES International Seminar on Problems of Planning in Eastern Europe, Tremezzo, Italy, July 1967, mimeographed, p. 4).

If it is assumed that *CED* in Figure 5 represents a locus of optimal sets of rules designed to allow maximum productivity (from given resources and technology) for each given number of rules,[10] then an economy located at point x can increase its productivity by (1) a vertical movement to the production frontier achieved by reform of the existing rules without changing their number and (2) a movement along the production frontier to *E* achieved by a successful search for the optimum number and combination of rules. If the search is not successful, the economy might end up at x' for example. Similarly, an economy at y can increase its productivity by reform of the existing rules (without changing their number) and a decrease in their number while improving the quality of the set.

This effort to construct a production frontier with respect to the number and quality of rules instead of technology and resources has been purposeful and not fanciful. Perhaps all over the world the most important factor determining the productivities of economies is the system of rules under which they operate. In an economy favored with resources and rapid technological development, the reduction of productivity due to a non-optimum set of rules may not be obvious. However, one can suggest that the non-market criteria governing Soviet-type economies result in a substantial reduction of the productivity of those systems without encountering opposition, at least not from Soviet and East European economists.

Let *CD* in Figure 6 represent the production frontier of the United States and *FG* that of the Soviet Union at the present point in time. *CD* lies above *FG* because of the current superiority in the existing capacity, capital accumulation, technology, and so forth, of the United States. If the economy of the United States is at point a, for example, and that of the Soviet Union at point s, both can attain a higher productivity simply by reform of non-market criteria without any increase in existing technology and resources. This specific example cannot be pushed too far because non-market criteria in the Soviet Union are products of an effort to replace rather than supplement market criteria, and it is on this basis that the Soviet economy has been considered to be a planned economy.

10. For each number of rules, there are a number of possible sets arrayed from the rules axis vertically to CED. Thus, for any given number of rules, there is a progression through better sets of rules from zero productivity to maximum productivity.

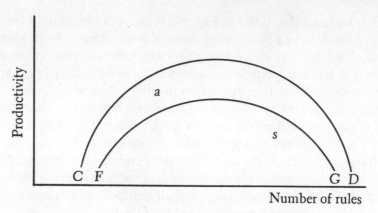

FIGURE 6.

The analysis in this chapter points to a problem in the literature which attempts to classify economic systems according to the laissez-faire—central planning spectrum of Figure 7. This literature seems to regard polycentric and hierarchic organization as the polar ends of the spectrum with "mixed economy" in between. It implies that polycentricity and hierarchy shade into one another as the amount of public ownership and number of rules are varied. By implication, this literature defines the organizational structures of a market system and a centrally planned system in terms of non-organizational criteria common to each: moving along the spectrum from left to right, replacing private with public ownership and simultaneously increasing the number of rules that circumscribe managers' autonomous choices of production functions, is believed to turn a market economy into a planned economy.

Thinking in terms of the spectrum of Figure 7 obscures the importance of the quality of non-market criteria, thus preventing a

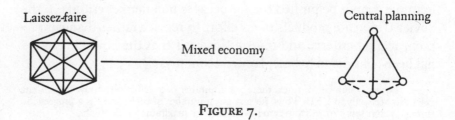

FIGURE 7.

vision of reform in terms of no net increase in the number of rules and instead fostering the association of reform with increased intervention or quantity of rules. It also obscures the fact that the number of rules (or extent of non-market criteria) is relevant to the *efficiency* of operation rather than to the *structure* of economic organization. More importantly, such thinking does not allow a clear differentiation between overall planning and central or administrative planning. The proper aim of overall planning is to devise rules or non-market criteria that lubricate the workings of a market system and increase its productivity. Overall planning and a market system are congruencies. Central planning has aimed at the elimination of market organization. Its goal was to organize the whole economy hierarchically as if it were a single factory.

Nature of Hierarchic Organization

Introduction: There is a new approach to theorizing about economic systems that any effort to discuss hierarchic organization must take into account. The concept of hierarchy brings to mind the concept of authority, and some recent analysts have rejected any approach based on the authority concept because they cannot define authority. Instead, they focus on informational differences between economic systems. In acknowledging difficulty in defining authority, they are on firm ground. For example, Simon states that "there is no consensus today in the management literature as to how the term 'authority' should be used."[11]

However, we know that an administrative or hierarchical structure possesses authority whether or not we can define authority, and we know that the function of a hierarchy is not simply communicating information. For example, Simon states that

> of all the modes of influence, authority is the one that chiefly distinguishes the behavior of individuals as participants of organizations from their behavior outside such organizations. *It is authority that gives an organization its formal structure,* and the other modes of influence may best be discussed after this structure has been specified.[12]

11. Herbert A. Simon, *Administrative Behavior*, 2nd ed. (New York: Macmillan, 1957), p. xxxiv.
12. Ibid., p. 124 (italics added).

Therefore, even if analysts succeed in defining the organizational structures of economic systems, rather than their optimality properties, in terms of unique informational differences, they will not have avoided the phenomenon of authority whatever their terminology.

In what follows I do not attempt to define such terms as "authority," "coordination," and "responsibility." I simply postulate that such phenomena exist independently of man's ability to formulate a precise and general definition of them. I do not argue that the marginal cost of administration increases indefinitely with size. My analysis of hierarchy is not a cost analysis but a *possibility* analysis and, thereby, allows going beyond Beckmann[13] to a more general consideration. What this section will show is that whatever the span of control and whatever the number of administrative levels, there is a definite limit to the number of tasks that hierarchic organization can coordinate per time period. Therefore, unless the span of control is infinite, a task of a definite size and complexity can always be imagined that is beyond the coordinative powers of hierarchic organization. Therefore, whatever the behavior of the marginal cost of administration, my argument holds for any finite span of control.

This section also shows the organizational structure of hierarchy and, thereby, the organizational structure of non-commodity modes of production. The identification of non-commodity modes of production with hierarchic organization might seem controversial. However, if we look for historical examples of non-commodity modes of production that are not hierarchical, we cannot readily find them. Karl Polanyi and his students and associates find that primitive and archaic economies and the economies of early empires were not characterized by production for sale on the market. They have found that "all economic systems known to us up to the end of feudalism in Western Europe were organized either on the principles of reciprocity or redistribution, or householding, or some combination of the three."[14] The historical examples of redistribution and householding are generally hierarchical. Economies organized by the

13. Martin J. Beckmann, "Some Aspects of Returns to Scale in Business Administration," *The Quarterly Journal of Economics*, vol. LXXIV, no. 3 (August 1960), pp. 464-71.
14. George Dalton, ed., *Primitive, Archaic, and Modern Economies* (New York: Doubleday Anchor, 1968), p. 18.

principle of redistribution are usually organized under a ruler or a priesthood to serve the perpetuation of the society and its purposes. Householding is organization under a family head. Reciprocity might appear to offer exceptions to hierarchical organization; however, the hierarchical character of an economy characterized by reciprocity derives from social custom.

In the context of an exposition of the implications of Marx's ideas, the identification of non-commodity modes of production with hierarchic organization is hardly controversial. Although Marx may have thought there had been historical examples of non-hierarchical non-commodity modes, he generally emphasizes the individual's subordination to the community as a characteristic of non-commodity modes. In his *Pre-capitalist Economic Formations*, non-commodity modes of production such as the Asiatic and the feudal are hierarchical.

When Marx talks about "associations of free individuals who work with jointly owned means of production," he usually implies or states that these cooperative efforts will be unified under a plan or by "one commanding will, and this performs a function, which does not refer to fragmentary operations, but to the combined labor of the workshop, in the same way as does that of a director of an orchestra."[15] By the "association of free individuals" Marx means men free from domination by productive relations that are of their own making, i.e., free from domination by the market. Marx argues that labor was freed by the market system from subordination to, or domination by, personal relations only to be dominated by the new productive relations (commodity production) associated with the freedom of labor from community or lord. Therefore, freedom requires liberation from the market and the use of a different organizing principle by which to integrate the economy and by which to establish control over it.

It is not necessary to argue that Marx unambiguously advocated a hierarchically organized economy for the future society. There simply was no alternative to his followers as the chaos of "workers' control" in Russia demonstrated. Workers' control may have had as a part of its foundation the misreading of Marx's "association of free individuals" by some of the revolutionaries. However that may be,

15. Karl Marx, *Capital*, vol. III (Chicago: Charles Kerr, 1909), p. 451.

it can be seen as an effort at workers' operation of factories free of central command. It soon became apparent that in the absence of a market system unifying the factories, central direction was required. It was realized, consciously or tacitly, that workers could operate factories free from central direction only if the factories were related in a market system (commodity production). Workers' control without a market system is not a viable or possible organizational system. Once an economy is characterized by complexity, democratic discussion among large numbers of workers is not sufficient to integrate the economy. In order to avoid integration through the market (commodity production), central planning was attempted.

Non-commodity modes of production are characterized by division of labor receiving its rationality either by (1) social custom as in a ritual economy, (2) administratively specified allocation as in a firm, or (3) a social plan as in a planned economy, and not by market exchange. Marx writes that the "division of labour is a necessary condition for the production of commodities, but it does not follow conversely that the production of commodities is a necessary condition for the division of labour. In the primitive Indian community there is a social division of labour, without production of commodities. Or, to take an example nearer home, in every factory the labour is divided according to a system, but this division is not brought about by the operatives mutually exchanging their individual products."[16] Marx thus defines the organization of production within a ritual economy and within the firm as examples of non-commodity modes, and, thereby, he associates non-commodity modes of production with hierarchic organization. Speaking of the future, Marx defines the organization of production within the socialist society in terms of a non-commodity mode of production. Marx writes that "the life-process of society, which is based on the process of material production, does not strip off its mystical veil until it is treated as production by freely associated men [men who are not alienated and who are not acting independently of one another], and is consciously regulated by them in accordance with a settled plan."[17]

Thus, Marx's approach to the classification of economic systems

16. Karl Marx, *Capital*, vol. I (Modern Library; New York: Random House, 1906), p. 49.
17. Ibid., p. 92.

allows unambiguous differentiation in terms of organizational structures. Marx explicitly defines and reviles capitalism as a commodity mode of production and explicitly defines future socialist society in terms of a non-commodity mode of production guided by a consciously formulated social plan. It is true that Marx was tight-lipped about *how* the socialist society would make its plan, but he did define the character of the organization of production under socialism.

Hierarchy: The basic characteristic of a hierarchic system is that its members are organized under the authority and responsibility of an ultimate superior. However decentralized the system, there remain lines of command flowing from an ultimate authority who bears the ultimate responsibility. Therefore, this chapter will analyze the structure and character of simple hierarchy.

The structure of hierarchy must be examined to see its function. Its structure is suitable for organizing a task, the interdependence of which can be subdivided into job assignments at descending levels of authority, finally reaching the subordinates, whether soldiers in the field or workers on the assembly line, at the base of the pyramid who are engaged directly in physical production rather than in organization and coordination. A task thus consists of the totality of the job assignments that comprise it. The structure of hierarchy indicates that it is the appropriate organizational form for tasks that can be centrally planned and coordinated. Individual job assignments come from above with instructions governing their implementation. The outcome is *ex ante* determined, although it can be frustrated by failure, and the primary function of superiors is to organize and coordinate their subordinates toward the achievement of the *ex ante* plan.

Since each person's job is centrally assigned and coordinated, a person's direct contacts are limited to his immediate superior and subordinates. Other direct contacts would short-circuit or sever lines of authority on which the organization relies. Diagrammatically (Figure 8), a direct contact between p and S would sever the line of authority connecting p to B and frustrate B's ability to coordinate p, q, and r. Similarly, direct contact between r and x obscures the authority and responsibility of B and C. That is why r and x, for example, are related to each other only through S. That is, the coordination of p, q, and r to x, y, and z is achieved by S through instructions given to B

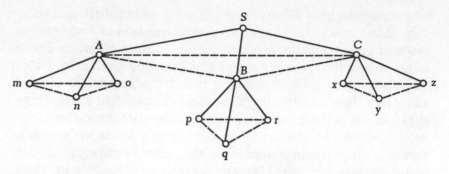

FIGURE 8.

and C. Although S may exhaust himself coordinating A, B, and C, he coordinates A, B, and C with a view toward the ultimate coordination of m, n, o, p, q, r, x, y, and z. Let the character of hierarchic coordination be clearly noted: hierarchy is coordinated by an ultimate superior in terms of aggregations of superior-subordinate groupings.[18]

Although hierarchy is a command structure, generally job assignments cannot be made in such detail that the actions of a subordinate are completely determined by his superior. Therefore, successful operation of hierarchy depends on an element of mutual adjustment among members within each superior-subordinate grouping and upon some interpretation of rules and instructions. A subordinate must use his initiative in how he carries through his job assignment. However, there is a definite limit to the extent of mutual adjustment and autonomous initiative. Mutual adjustment and autonomous initiative may condition the actions of subordinates in carrying out job assignments but must not determine them. In order for a superior to remain responsible for coordination of his subordinates' activities, he must remain decisive in determining their undertakings.

Hierarchy can be expanded in two ways: (1) by an increase in the span of control and (2) by increasing the height of the pyramid through the addition of new levels. We will examine expansion by each method in turn. The argument is that there are natural limits to the coordinative powers of hierarchy. Just as the statement that

18. A superior-subordinate grouping is defined diagrammatically (Figure 8) as S, A, B, C or A, m, n, o.

"it is impossible for a cat to swim the Atlantic" does not require qualification in terms of the calmness of the ocean and the presence or absence of sharks, the statement that there are natural limits to the coordinative powers of hierarchic organization is independent of the quality of supervisors, the obedience of subordinates, the quality, cost, and flow of information, the problem of sanctions, and so forth. Although such factors are of great practical importance and limit the effectiveness of any hierarchy, even a hierarchy with excellent information and perfectly obedient subordinates faces limits to its coordinative powers. Focusing on factors such as the quality of personnel and information, willful distortion, and lags between levels has apparently given some the idea that if imperfections are removed, there would be no limits to hierarchic coordination. Therefore, some have argued that theoretically a centrally planned economy is conceivable. I do not agree with that, if there are a large number of possible outputs and production functions subject to significant rates of change as in a modern economy. That is why the argument here emphasizes natural limits to hierarchic coordination, and is not based on practical considerations that reduce the effectiveness of hierarchic organization.

In Figure 8 the span of control is three. Therefore, to coordinate the job assignments of his subordinates, each superior must adjust three relations. For example, S must adjust A to B, A to C, and B to C. The adjustment must be performed anew each time there is a change in conditions requiring recoordination. If the span of control is increased by one to four, in order to coordinate the actions of four subordinates, A, B, C, and D, a superior has six relations to adjust. He must coordinate A to B, A to C, A to D, B to C, B to D, and C to D.[19] In this case adding one subordinate doubles the number of relations a superior must coordinate. In general, the number of relations r to be coordinated is $s/2 \, (s-1)$, where s is the span of control. Thus, since the number of relations between subordinates requiring adjustment goes up steeply with the number of subordinates (Table I), there is a definite limit to the expansion of hierarchy by increasing the span of control. For any given ability of a superior and rate of

19. In coordinating A to B, the superior is simultaneously coordinating B to A. Although there is but one relation to be adjusted between two participants, two orders are required—one to A and one to B.

TABLE I

increase in s	s	r	increase in r
	3	3	
1			3
	4	6	
1			4
	5	10	
1			5
	6	15	
	—	—	
	10	45	
1			10
	11	55	

change in conditions, as s increases a number is reached at which r exceeds the controlling powers of his mind. *Ceteris paribus*, the model predicts a larger s in cases of routine or standardized coordinative jobs subject to low rates of change and a smaller s in cases of non-standardized coordinative jobs subject to high rates of change.

Holding the span of control constant, expansion by increasing the height of the pyramid through the addition of new levels does not allow a hierarchy to expand appreciably the tasks it can coordinate per time period. With a task defined in terms of the totality of the job assignments that comprise it, and with job assignments being (1) coordinative in nature for every member of the hierarchy who is someone else's superior and (2) directly productive in nature for those on the lowest level, the argument can be illustrated mathematically as follows.

In order to coordinate one relation, a superior must issue a minimum of two orders, one to each party involved. The maximum number of orders c that a superior can issue per time period will depend on his ability, the complexity of his coordinative job, and the amount of time and effort he must give to finding and using information and so forth to carry out his job. Let c be determined. Then

$$(1) \quad r = c/2 = s/2 \, (s-1)$$

$$(2) \quad s = \frac{1 + (1 + 4c)^{\frac{1}{2}}}{2}.$$

Since, by definition, a hierarchic system exists only if $s \geq 2$, it must be possible that $c \geq 2$ if the hierarchy is to function.

If each superior is assumed to have a span of control s that is fully utilized throughout, each lower level will have s times as many persons as the level above it. If the number of levels is L, the total number of persons comprised will be

(3) $\quad p = 1 + s + s^2 + \ldots + s^{L-1} = \dfrac{s^L - 1}{s - 1}.$

A hierarchy accomplishes its task by the coordination of the activities of those at the base of the pyramid. For semantic convenience, we assume that to achieve a task per year, coordination must occur yearly, where a "year" is any arbitrary period of time. The maximum yearly orders that can be issued are $c(p - s^{L-1})$, and these must coordinate $ar(s^{L-2})$ relations at the base of the pyramid. Hence the maximum number of yearly tasks (t) will be

(4) $\quad t = \dfrac{c(p - s^{L-1})}{2r(s^{L-2})}, L \geq 2, c \geq 2.$

Since $r = {}^s/_2 (s - 1)$ and $(p - s^{L-1}) = \dfrac{s^{L-1} - 1}{s - 1}$,

(5) $\quad t = \dfrac{c(s^{L-1} - 1)}{s^{L-1}(s - 1)^2}$

(6) $\quad = c(s - 1)^{-2} (1 - s^{1-L}), L \geq 2, c \geq 2.$

Differentiating, we find

(7) $\quad \dfrac{\partial t}{\partial L} = c(s - 1)^{-2} s^{1-L} \ln s, \ \ln s > 0.$

Finally, if c and hence s remain fixed,

(8) $\quad \lim_{L \to \infty} t = c(s - 1)^{-2} = 2c[1 + 2c - (1 + 4c)^{\frac{1}{2}}]^{-1}$

(9) $\quad \lim_{L \to \infty} \dfrac{\partial t}{\partial L} = 0$

$$(10) \quad \frac{1}{t} \left[\lim_{\substack{L \to \infty \\ L=2}} t \right] = s(s-1)^{-1} = \left[(1+4c)^{\frac{1}{2}} + 1 \right] \left[(1+4c)^{\frac{1}{2}} - 1 \right]^{-1}.$$

It follows that there is a definite limit to the number of tasks a hierarchy can achieve yearly, a limit reached by expanding the levels in the hierarchy indefinitely. The maximum multiple in yearly tasks is given by equation (10). For example, with $c = 2$ and hence $s = 2$, t rises from 1 to 2 when L is increased from 2 to infinity: yearly tasks can be doubled; but with $c = 72$ and hence $s = 9$, t rises from 1 to only 1.125 as L is increased from 2 to infinity.

If non-coordinative activities of superiors are to expand along with the expansion of the pyramid, c must decline as L increases, the one effect on multiplication of tasks offsetting the other, although we cannot predict the precise net effect.

Market Signals

Perhaps because they considered scarcity a product of the capitalistic distribution of income, those who shared the Marxian aspirations overlooked the allocative problem of operating either an industrial economy or a large national economy without market signals. A peasant community producing for its direct use does not face the problem because its possible output mix is very limited and so are its possible production functions, and the alternatives can be weighed in a man's mind. However, the rational operation of an economy in which there are a large number of production possibilities according to decisions "taken directly by the planning authority, which balances means and ends by one act of judgment, as an individual acting without economic relationships does"[20] would require a mental span of control greatly in excess of any humanly attainable. By reviewing, although in a brief and simplified manner, functions of price and profit movements, the plight of a Marxian central planning board comes into focus.

In Figure 9a, the supply curve (S_1) represents various rates of output for a given capacity. As the level of demand rises, a higher price calls forth increasing rates of output. If the increase in the level of

20. R. L. Hall, *The Economic System in a Socialist State* (London: Macmillan, 1937), p. 233.

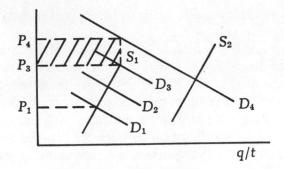

FIGURE 9a.

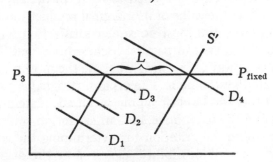

FIGURE 9b.

demand outstrips possible rates of output, an inelastic supply will be rationed by pure price rises. In the case of a factor of production, we know the factor will tend to be allocated where the value of its marginal product is highest as determined by consumer preferences through derived demand.[21]

The pure price rises—unaccompanied by an increase in the rate of output—result in pure profit, which is the signal to expand, that is, to shift the supply curve to the right. The amount of the shift is related to profitability, and relative expansions are determined by relative profitabilities. In this way the growth (and decline) of firms and industries is governed by consumer preferences. Whatever this means, it does mean that productive relations throughout the economy are related to each other and that outputs are related to needs. For instance, producers of nails are not rewarded if their output mix is badly related or unrelated to the production functions or needs of

21. This results whether the preferences are "natural" or "contrived."

others. This tendency holds whatever its approximation to some theoretical "optimum."

We can realize the functions and meaning of price and profit movements by observing the situation in their absence. For instance, let the price be fixed at P_3 (Figure 9b). Once the level of demand increases beyond D_3, a result of the fixed price is an artificial shortage such as L, making necessary some non-price rationing criteria by which to determine the allocation between the demanders (or to its uses). We know that although there are exceptions, generally such criteria are arbitrary with regard to fairness and that it would be purely coincidental if the criteria tended to result in the allocation of the resource to where the value of its marginal product was highest or to where it produced the most consumer satisfaction. Generally, the most productive users can pay the highest price, but if the price is fixed, there is no way of knowing what are the most productive uses.

There is another problem. The expansion signal is blocked. It can be observed that the level of supply is not adequate given the level of demand and the fixed price, and an expansion could be ordered. But what is to be the criterion for determining the amount of increase in capacity? A possibility suggested by the diagram (Figure 9b) is a shift to S', but that would be determining growth according to an arbitrary shortage resulting from an arbitrarily fixed price. If the price had been fixed at any other point, the resulting shortage would have been greater or less. Use of such a criterion results in expansion unrelated to relative profitability and in outputs badly related to needs.

Imagine n producers, n being a very large number, all in the situation of Figure 9b. Imagine a central planning board faced with the problem of determining relative expansions. By what criteria can the n relative expansions be determined? If the central planning board seeks to avoid the problem by ordering all n expansions to S', it will find it has not sufficient resources and will have to ration the available resources for expansion according to some criteria. Whatever the criteria might be, no one knows what they are, and their meaning is more in doubt than the meaning of the profitability criterion.

Except for the case of public goods, which are relatively few in number, any criteria for priority rationing other than profitability are ultimately arbitrary, as many economists throughout the Soviet

Union and Eastern Europe now maintain. Whereas it is possible for an economy to function by non-profit-determined expansion, not only is the meaning of the output in question, but eventually there will be a shortage of storage space for production unrelated to wants. If consumer preferences are turned to as the solution for such wastage, it may be discovered that some of the capacity that has been constructed and represented as economic growth is unprofitable.

If the "central planning board" orders expansion in keeping with relative profitability and allocates resources in keeping with price signals, it is a redundant entity, absorbing resources in a simulation of what would tend to happen in its absence. Although such a "central planning board" might aim at taking into account externalities and at simulating the purely competitive model (if such an attempt is conceivable), in order to avoid theoretical imperfections and worry over monopoly, rather than aim at simulating a real-world market economy, the cost of doing so would have to be taken into account before it could be asserted that people would be better off. Furthermore, the aim of such a simulation would be to achieve by the use of theoretical market principles a better market equilibrium than a real-world market achieves and, thereby, is not classifiable as central economic planning unless we define, as at least one economist has done, the achievement of competitive equilibrium and central economic planning as equal. Such a definition implies a classificatory scheme in which the theoretical classification of economic systems is according neither to their outcomes (equal) nor to the principles by which they operate (equal).[22]

22. See Chapter 5.

CHAPTER 4

The Polycentric Soviet Economy

Economists have not been able to understand both the market economy and the Soviet economy in terms of their theoretical apparatus. They think of the market in terms of the principles of economic efficiency and cannot account for the operation of the Soviet economy in terms of its reflecting the principles of economic efficiency, and they think of the Soviet economy as a planned economy and cannot account for hierarchic organization in terms of economic theory. Economists working with measures of economic growth and tools of marginal analysis and economists who focus on informational differences between economic systems or follow the "adjustment process" approach[1] to comparative economic systems are unable to construct a theory that takes into account the uniqueness of the Soviet economy. Likewise, the field of theoretical economic systems in general has got scarcely anywhere. Existing models of central planning, market socialism, and market capitalism can in theory all achieve or approach the marginal conditions for economic efficiency, leaving economists confused as to the significant differences in their theoretical models. As a result, the Soviet economy is usually compared to a market economy in terms of growth rate, degree of consumer freedom, property rights, and relative efficiency. The half-century-old effort in the Soviet Union first to avoid in theory and practice "commodity production" and now to return to it,

1. See, for example, Leonid Hurwicz, "Optimality and Informational Efficiency in Resource Allocation Processes" in *Mathematical Methods in the Social Sciences, 1959,* edited by Arrow, Karlin, and Suppes (Stanford: Stanford University Press, 1960), pp. 27-46.

although noticed by sovietologists in terms of the Soviet discussion of the applicability of the "law of value" under socialism, remains unnoticed by the field of comparative economic systems.

Sovietologists have noted that in the Soviet Union a major part of the activity of the planning apparatus goes into the effort to supply firms with inputs. They are aware that notorious failures in supply and work stoppages are results of this activity. Reform-minded economists in the Soviet Union have criticized the planning apparatus for devoting substantial resources that could go into the preparation of more consistent and rational plans to an effort to act as supply agents for firms. Some Western economists have also criticized the Soviet planning apparatus for a misdirection of its efforts and have argued that the failure to decentralize the supply apparatus for industrial materials is a primary source of inefficiency in the Soviet economy. Although some Soviet and Western economists have noticed the faults of the supply efforts of the planning apparatus and criticized the procedure as a misdirection of the planners' efforts, no one has explained why the planning apparatus has traditionally engaged in this activity that is so costly to the economy. They seem simply to accept it as a hallmark of the irrationality of central planning as practiced in the Soviet Union.

Much progress is made possible just by the simple realization that Marx classifies economic systems according to those that produce commodities and those that do not. Whatever the fruitfulness of approaching comparative economic systems from the standpoints of informational flows, growth rates, and mathematical formulations of optimality conditions, they are not historical approaches to the theoretical study of economic systems. The aim of that central planning which has been a historical force is to eliminate market organization (commodity production), and this aim has its origin in Marx. Therefore, the historically interesting criteria for the classification of economic systems are Marx's. With these criteria the relationship of Marxism to socialist planning and the Soviet economy is historically defined.

By following Marx's approach to the classification of economic systems, we discover the origin of socialist planning (whether or not the Soviet Union any longer consciously recognizes its original purpose) and can discuss economic organization without reference to the conditions for economic efficiency. Marx, of course, discussed the organization of the commodity mode of production, that is, the market system, with no reference to Pareto optimal conditions. There is a clarity in Marx's approach that is missing from the modern approach. Specifically, Marx's approach allows recognition that a simulation of the commodity mode of production remains a commodity mode of production and prevents any abstract approaches to the study of economic systems that do not reflect the actual material processes. Theorizing is permitted, but it must bear on real economic processes or otherwise it is "idealistic" or a purely mental conception. The theorizing that envisages scientific socialists solving millions of simultaneous equations and producing the "optimal plan" is purely romantic and verges on fantasy. However, even the serious scholarly efforts suffer in that they either do not bear on reality or they misrepresent commodity production and polycentric economic processes as socialist planning and hierarchy. For example, one might say to Hurwicz[2] that optimizing on the basis of informational flows is remote from the motivations that are historically fundamental to the concept of socialist planning and suffers as an approach to comparative systems because it does not deal directly with the structures of organizational systems but with optimality properties. And one might say to Peter Wiles that his "perfect administration" or "perfect computation" model of central planning has a misleading name because its essential feature is that it works by eliminating completely the need for an administrative structure in which decisions are made and achieves "perfection" by simulating the competitive model. To regard the autonomous results of the competitive process as a set of "commands" to be issued to productive units is to overlook the fact that the simulation of the market reflects the polycentric structure of the market and the commodity mode of production rather than the structure of hierarchy. In such theories of planning, the central planning board is, like Walras's auctioneer, merely an announcer of information. The planning board has no purposive intent. It receives "plans" as givens from the simulation of the market and announces them. The only purpose such a procedure could have is to achieve better by theoretical market principles what the market would actu-

2. Ibid.

ally achieve. Such a process bears no relationship to the aspirations of socialist planning.

As a result of his investigations, Campbell postulates that "the structure of production relationships is not hierarchical."[3] This postulate means that if economic theory reflects the structure of production relationships and the structure of production relationships is not hierarchical, then economic theory does not reflect hierarchical relationships.[4] Therefore, any effort to construct a theory of planning in terms of economic theory will be beset with contradiction.[5]

As I have suggested elsewhere,[6] it would seem that in a centrally planned economy theory and practice must merge. If planners do not know how they are operating their economy, it is incongruous to describe such an economy as centrally planned. In a centrally planned economy, the blueprint of the economy's operation would be the theory of central planning. Ames writes that no theory of the Soviet economy exists and that he believes the Soviets "have even less explicit theory about their own economy than western Sovietologists."[7] A market economy can operate without anyone knowing how and, indeed, did so for a long time; that is, knowledge of its operation is not essential to its operation, although knowledge of its operation may allow improvement through policy. However, by definition, a centrally planned economy operates according to the conscious designs of men. If the Soviets have less than no theory about central planning and less idea about how their economy operates than Western sovietologists, it would seem that the Soviet economy is essentially an autonomous economy. Such a conclusion appears less risky than

3. Robert Campbell, "On the Theory of Economic Administration" in *Industrialization in Two Systems*, edited by Henry Rosovsky (New York: Wiley, 1966), p. 194.

4. Noting years ago that the structure of modern production was not hierarchical, Michael Polanyi derived the principle that the structure of economic organization must reflect the nature of the task, i.e., if the task is polycentric in nature, it cannot be governed by hierarchic organization and vice versa. From this principle he concluded that central planning in the Marxist sense was impossible and that the Soviet economy was not centrally planned. Instead, it was a "disguised market economy" by which he meant that the normal economic rationality of a market economy was distorted by the effort to subordinate polycentric processes to a hierarchic structure.

5. See Chapter 5.

6. Paul Craig Roberts, "Drewnowski's Economic Theory of Socialism," *The Journal of Political Economy*, vol. 76, no. 4, part I (July/August 1968), pp. 645-50.

7. Edward Ames, *Soviet Economic Processes* (Homewood, Ill.: Irwin, 1965), pp. 1, 3.

postulating that in the Soviet Union a centrally planned economy exists independently of the consciousness of the central planners.

Ames offers a theoretical understanding of what is going on in the Soviet economy, *but he does not offer his theory as being a procedure consciously followed by planners.* Ames's theory might allow prediction of Soviet economic results and thereby may be useful, but the theory is not *true* because it does not bear on reality in the sense of accounting for the motivation of the effort to plan centrally in the Soviet Union.

Since Ames's attempt to provide a theory of Soviet planning is based on his study of the Soviet economy, it is interesting that his theory does not comprise a planning procedure. This is evidence of the contradiction in the effort to construct a theory of planning in terms of economic theory and/or evidence that the nature of Soviet economic reality is different from the classification of it as planned. Ames treats plans as constraints on the autonomy of managers, not as assigned functions to be achieved. He has Soviet firms maximizing outputs rather than profits, but in his theory Soviet firms are not essentially less autonomous than Western firms. Given certain restraints, Soviet enterprises decide their output mixes, their rates of outputs, and in many instances, through their own investment policies, their levels of outputs. Ames does not show that the "plans" are *planned as constraints* designed to produce an output predetermined by central planners, that is, that the "plans" comprise a set of coordinated orders designed to achieve some objective.

The voluminous writings on central economic planning over a period of six decades have failed to discover a procedure for centrally deriving economic plans by which to organize the economy. Yet, respectable accounts of the Soviet economy by Western scholars presuppose that a central process of plan derivation exists and that the plans so derived organize and control economic activity. Curiously, in these accounts the plans are taken as given. Discussion and theorizing begin after the act of planning (which if it exists, should be explained) is accepted as a given datum. Bergson, for example, never describes the process for deriving the structure of output.[8] Instead, planning has come to be associated with attempts to supply

8. Abram Bergson, *The Economics of Soviet Planning* (New Haven: Yale University Press, 1964).

enterprises with inputs consistent with their productive capacity. No doubt the composition of output is influenced by priority rationing, but studies of the material-balances process indicate that such rationing operates more on the margin than on the whole. The problem of central planning is to find a central process for the rational ex ante derivation of the structure of output for the entire economy. This is not even attempted by the material-balances process.

Scholars do not seem to be bothered by the absence of a theory of how the structure of output is derived. A representative description of economic planning in the Soviet economy is given by Loucks:

> Economic planning in the Soviet economy neither implies a willingness to accept the totality of the results of the decisions of separate economic units and then call this a "plan," nor proceeds by projecting trends into the future and then developing the details of the plan around these. . . .
>
> Nor does Soviet planning consist of pushing trend lines into the future and then labeling them economic plans. Rather, its essence is the choosing of comprehensive goals and the apportioning to the separate economic units of the specific tasks involved in achieving these goals.[9]

Soviet economists engaged in economic reform seem to have a totally different view of economic planning in the Soviet economy. Liberman had written three years previously in the September 9, 1962 issue of Pravda that "in actuality, the plans of enterprises are set according to the so-called 'record basis,' that is, proceeding from the level attained."[10]

These two descriptions appear contradictory, and Liberman's description does not seem consistent with what we usually mean by central economic planning. Such contradictory descriptions result, perhaps, from the fact that the Soviet economy is supposed to be a planned economy, and scholars have had neither an alternative framework from which to view the Soviet economy nor principles on which to build an alternative framework. Our efforts to understand theoretically the operation of the Soviet economy have been hampered by

9. William N. Loucks, Comparative Economic Systems, 7th ed. (New York: Harper, 1965), pp. 543-44.

10. Yevsei G. Liberman, "The Plan, Profits, and Bonuses," as translated in Current Digest of the Soviet Press, vol. XIV, no. 36 (October 3, 1962), p. 15.

both the effort to fit it into a framework of hierarchical planning and the neglect of the original aspirations of Marxian socialism.

Having shown fundamental difficulties in present approaches to theorizing about the Soviet economic system, we offer a different approach.

Not many people are particularly satisfied with our understanding of the functioning of the Soviet economic system. An unclear understanding may be due to a lack of information. However, there is evidence that in "Soviet-type" economies planners and economists themselves, who would be expected to have the actual blueprint of the functioning of the planned economy, do not understand clearly the functioning of their systems.[11] This suggests that at least part of the problem may be one of classification.

One of the most difficult and most important problems in science is that of classification. Our heritage of scientific thinking has taught us that different characteristics of seemingly different phenomena do not prevent us from deciding that what we find common between them is more important to their classification than obvious differences. Scientific classification is a judgment skill requiring great qualitative discernment and is thereby subject to high risk of error. However, the classification of the Soviet economy as centrally planned seems to be based more on the acceptance of a claim than on any great mental effort and scientific discussion of its classification, and it has not resulted in any great amount of clarity about the functioning of the system.

Out of dissatisfaction with our theoretical understanding of the actual functioning of the Soviet economy and in the spirit of hoping to generate for the first time a scientific discussion over the classification of the Soviet economy, I suggest that a more productive way of viewing the Soviet economy might be to see it as a polycentric system[12] with signals that are irrational from the standpoint of eco-

11. Jan Drewnowski ("The Economic Theory of Socialism: A Suggestion for Reconsideration," *Journal of Political Economy*, vol. LXIX, no. 4 [August 1961]), for example, writes that the rational core of Soviet-type economies is difficult to detect.

12. Recently Dr. Edwin G. Dolan (Dartmouth College) has forcefully advanced this argument by building a formal model and experimenting with computer simulations. His work is an important demonstration that Soviet economic organization is characterized by polycentricity. See "An Experimental Polycentric Model of the Soviet Economy" (unpublished article).

nomic efficiency. This is not to suggest that the Soviet government is guilty of conscious misrepresentation of the actual character of the economy. Neither is this to suggest that Western scholars cannot see beyond Soviet propaganda. To classify the Soviet economy as polycentric does seem to fly in the face of the facts.

For instance, we know from reliable accounts that Soviet enterprises receive the most detailed instructions which seem to circumscribe completely their decisions, leaving no room even for maneuver in how they carry out their assigned tasks, much less allowing the enterprises control over the structures of their outputs. The existence of these detailed instructions is a fact, and in the face of this fact the suggestion that the Soviet economy is polycentric appears absurd.

However, the standard interpretation of the fact of detailed instructions is very misleading. The Hungarian economist Tibor Liska has written that

> as the number of directives to be observed increases, the more detailed and the stricter they become in a most intricate economic life hardly lending itself to standardization, the greater the liberty of individual planners and economic managers. The intricacy of economic life follows, namely, primarily from the fact that hosts of contrary tendencies must be brought into harmony with optimum efficiency. The stricter and more rigid the regulations prescribing the enforcement of such contrary tendencies, the more contradictory the directives must become. One receiving the directives has but a single choice: *not to observe all the directives*. On the other hand, in the decision to keep to one out of the necessarily contradictory directives, and drop the others, as well as in aiming at the issue of certain directives, he has a freedom almost greater than the most sovereign of tyrants.[13]

There is another widely observed fact that agrees with Liska's interpretation of the fact of detailed instructions. The planners do not know even what sort of nails or steam boilers will be produced. Such decisions are determined by the individual manager's interpretations of the "success indicators." The parallel in organizational terms is to the operation of a polycentric rather than hierarchic system. The dif-

13. Tibor Liska, "The Development of Market Relations and of the Theory and Practice of Price Mechanism in Socialism," Lecture at CESES International Seminar on Problems of Planning in Eastern Europe, Tremezzo, Italy, July 1967, mimeographed, p. 4.

ference lies in the quality or rationality of the signals that are interpreted.[14] The individual manager's interpretation of the "success
indicators" can result in his being rewarded even though his production satisfies no one but the statistician measuring it. The swelling
opposition in Eastern Europe and the Soviet Union to such wastage
of scarce resources testifies either that the plans cannot control the
structure of output or that the conscious purpose of the plans is to
waste scarce resources in lands not known for a surfeit of consumer
satisfaction.

We might pursue the question of the determination of the structure of output. One could accept that the outputs of enterprises for
any given year are *ex post* phenomena largely determined by managerial interpretation of "success indicators" and argue that this only
shows the difficulties of successfully implementing a central plan
and not the impossibility of deriving one. Failure or sabotage in plan
implementation does not explain away the plans themselves.

How are the plans derived? Michael Polanyi was the first to see
that the formula of plan derivation is the forecasting of a target for a
forthcoming few months by adding to the results of the previous
months a percentage increase. This view has been subject to some
ridicule in the past, but it has been borne out by Liberman's statement in *Pravda* quoted previously. Western experts on the Soviet
economy neglected the meaning of Liberman's statement. Instead,
they focused on his profit proposals for making "planning" more
efficient.

The published plans appear to be almost entirely composed of
forecasts[15] derived from what amounts to asking each enterprise its
ex ante production plans and negotiating over percentage increases.
The individual plans of each enterprise are then handed back to

14. There is another difference. Although the category of "price" in a market
economy does not change as a result of managerial interpretation, specific prices do
change. Likewise, the category of "success indicators" does not change as a result of
managerial interpretation, but in this case change in the specific signals, or the determination within the category of the specific indicators that serve as signals at points in time,
is not clearly a result of managerial interpretation as are changes in specific prices in a
market system. Changes in specific indicators have the appearance of being introduced
from above, though actually the changes are in response to the interpretation of prior
indicators made by managers.

15. The plan is changed so often that it is not congruous to say that it controls the
development of events in the economy. There is an alternative possibility that the development of events controls the plan.

them with instructions to perform them; and the bureaucracy then tries to supply each plant with the necessary inputs. Polanyi has pointed out that in such a case the initiative lies essentially with the enterprises since they have better knowledge of their productive capacity than does the center and that the plan issued from the center, often long after the process of production supposedly controlled by it has been underway, has the character of an aggregate of the individual plans originating in the enterprises.

The claims made for central economic planning are not as broad as they were even a few years ago. There is a general movement, East and West, to redefine it as the determination of new investment, and there is the fact of central control over investment in the Soviet Union. How can one reconcile this apparent fact with the contention that the Soviet economy operates as a polycentric rather than as a hierarchic system?

To prevent a red herring from being pulled across the trail, before suggesting what this central control might amount to, let me say that I accept unequivocally that the *structure* of the Soviet economy was decisively affected by the influence of a few central decisions, particularly those of Stalin, on the path of expansion of the production frontier. However, to influence the path of expansion is not to determine whether the economy functions hierarchically or polycentrically. It could be decided to outlaw the production of automobiles and this would decisively affect the structure of the economy of the United States, but the economy would remain a polycentric system.

A capital market can be replaced under conditions of public ownership by another polycentric form, one that is simply more clumsy and less efficient from an economic standpoint because it cannot take as full advantage of explicit productivity signals. It may or may not be true that each investment allocation would have to be ultimately approved by some supreme financial authority. However, these "supreme decisions" would be primarily determined by the requests of the various enterprises and ministries and by the arguments and pressures put forward by each in support of their rival claims. This interplay of rival pressure groups, each supported by its own combination of political and economic (and personal) arguments, is similar in its organization to the competition of enterprises or individuals for private capital.

The Eastern literature on planning generally makes it quite clear that it is impossible to construct a plan as was originally intended. What then is the function of the planning bureaucracy? Whatever the intention might be, in effect *the primary function of the planning bureaucracy is to act as supply agents for enterprises*[16] *in order to avoid free price formation and exchange on the market so that productive inputs will not have the appearance of commodities.* This satisfies the ideology underlying the whole effort at the expense of notorious failures in supply.

This argument is strengthened by taking into account the political power of the "planning" authority to intervene directly in the affairs of individual firms and its *inability* to intervene in the affairs of all firms simultaneously. In any "plan period" there will be a "crash-program" underway in which the operation of specific firms will be in accordance with direct intervention. Often the direct intervention disorganizes the economy by producing unexpected bottlenecks and certainly has an influence on overall economic activity. However, as Nutter has observed, it is the momentum of the vast remainder of the economy that carries matters along from day-to-day irrespective of central planning authorities.[17] The relationship between the overall autonomy of the economy and direct intervention by authority is indicated by Figure 10. The planning authority has the political power to intervene directly into the affairs of all firms, but only has the ability to exercise this power over a relatively few firms at a time.[18]

The major differences between Western economies and the Soviet economy are not in fundamental differences between the organiza-

16. This view seems to be supported by the conclusions of many of the reformers that the primary efforts of the planning bureaucracy are directed simply to achieve what could better be achieved by individual enterprises establishing their own supply lines on the basis of commercial relations. These reformers appear unaware that the heritage of their economy lies in the effort to eliminate commodity production.

17. G. Warren Nutter, "How Soviet Planning Works," *New Individualist Review*, vol. IV, no. 1 (summer 1965), pp. 20-25.

18. It might be argued that the "planning" authority plans the economy in stages. For example, in period 1 mining and transportation are planned, in period 2 steel production is planned, in period 3 production of products made from steel is planned, and so forth. Such an argument implies that factories using steel in their production must be idle during periods 1 and 2 and leaves open the question of the relationship of the planned sector to the overall economy. Mining and transportation, for example, cannot be planned separately from the rest of the economy. Any such approach would result in adjusting mining and transportation to the overall functioning and needs of the autonomous economy.

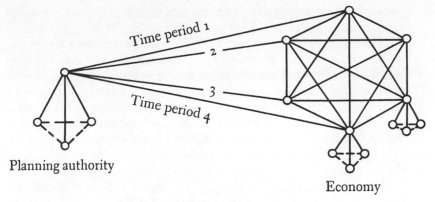

Planning authority

Economy

FIGURE 10.

tional structures of the systems—*the Soviet economy produces commodities just as do Western economies*—but in (1) the relationship of the political authority to the economy and (2) the relative efficiency of operation as determined by the relative efficiencies of (a) the signals on which the economies rely and (b) the ownership arrangements and non-market criteria. Although there are firms in Western economies that have experienced efforts of political authority to intervene directly in their affairs, the difference in (1) remains a difference in *kind* as well as a *political* difference. The origins of Soviet efforts at central planning are ideological, and the relationship of political to economic life in the Soviet Union reflects attempts to satisfy ideological passions.

Liska has reminded us recently that the most important condition for a new socialist-communist society was considered to be the liquidation of commodity production, but he argues that price and money relations theoretically condemned to liquidation have been extended under socialism at a pace more rapid than ever before in history. He writes that

the main practical trend of directive planned economy was an expansion of commodity and money relations.

Namely, directive planned economy is essentially a State inflation mechanism camouflaged by a bureaucracy of prices. In the case of free price movements, not even the most reckless floating of money can result in a general shortage, as prices may always rise to the higher level made realizable by a quicker turnover or growing quantity of money. In open inflation, the balance of demand and supply is attained again and again at a constantly increasing level of prices. But if, in order to avoid an inflation in prices, price rises are hindered by the State via administrative measures, demand aiming at a quicker turnover or showing in an increasing quantity of money can get even greater than the grand total price of goods supplied. In practice, this means standing in the queue for an ever greater number of goods. From the queues getting longer and longer, the situation would soon become that only those heading the line would be able to buy anything for their money if the State did not intercede with some kind of ration system, i.e., by the determination of material contingents between enterprises, manpower plans, investment and exchange frames, etc., for the distribution of shortage goods. The generalization of this practice is directive planned economy itself.[19]

Liska is offering another "window" through which to view Soviet-type economies.[20] Looking through Liska's window, we see the planning bureaucracy as directing its activities toward overcoming problems created by its own existence. For example, the Hungarian Price Office is made necessary by the other ministries spending money on investments that are not recovered. The increase in the money supply in this case results in a destruction of resources and not in an increase in production. "The greater the extent of an economically un-

19. Liska, "The Development of Market Relations," p. 4.
20. Liska's "window" is the window through which Michael Polanyi was looking twenty-two years previously. In *Full Employment and Free Trade* (London: Cambridge University Press, 1945), Polanyi argues that state controls in the Soviet Union that are regarded as constituting central economic planning had their origin in the attempt to counter an excessive monetary circulation by suppressing inflation and in measures taken by the authorities to deal with the disorganizing effects of inflation and suppressed inflation. At a time when it was claimed that central planning had solved the unemployment problem in the Soviet Union, Polanyi showed his superior insight in a strongly developed argument that full employment was established in Soviet Russia

simply by maintaining a budget deficit which kept the labour market under inflationary pressure. Compulsory labour regulations were adopted only, or mainly, in order to meet the difficulties of the excessive demand for labour created by the inflationary pressure. These measures, far from being responsible for the achievement of full employment, were, on the contrary, necessitated by an already established state of full or more than full employment which they had played no part in producing (p. 67).

Polanyi's intelligence was wasted on the milieu of his time, a milieu in which Keynesians had relegated the influence of the money supply on employment to insignificance and in which the supposition that a socialist centrally planned economy existed in the Soviet Union was upheld by widespread disaffection from the market.

justified spending of money," writes Liska, the greater the danger of
rapid inflation and "the more the choice is restricted to price bureaucracy." The function of administrative price-fixing is to suppress inflation, and the concept of "planned prices" loses its meaning. The
tendency has been to reject such arguments as Liska's for not fitting
the phenomenon as standardly classified, whereas the real problem
might be that the standard classification does not fit the phenomenon.

Bognar states explicitly that the system of plan directives and in-
dices in Hungary never accomplished anything more than to disor-
ganize what in an organizational sense remained a market economy.[21]
Concerning the theory of planned economy, Bognar writes: "It has
again been confirmed that wrong theories do not change reality, but
restrict and disorient the opportunities for rational human action."[22]
He writes that "the assumptions (calculations and prescriptions) of
the leadership essentially deviate from the actual economic processes."[23] He writes that the plan is insensitive to value relations and
thereby cannot control the economic process. He nowhere assumes
that the plan should or could determine these value relations. Rather,
he accepts as unquestionable that value relations are independent and
autonomous forces. Such statements as Bognar's, which are widespread in the Eastern literature, suggest that the natural structure of
the economic task of modern industrial society is inherently different
in kind from the structure of hierarchy.

In the past, we were armed with a rationale and a hope against
doubts about the Soviet economy. The rationale is that planned
economy has produced rapid industrialization, and the hope is that
the inefficiency will be overcome by advances in computers and
simulation techniques. Neither the rationale nor the hope any longer
appears meaningful. Many Hungarian, Czechoslovakian, and Yugo-
slavian economists are saying that they do not think much of the rapid
industrialization rationale. They say that the result of "planned
economy" was to produce a structure of capacity, much of which is
unprofitable, and that they do not consider the construction of unprofitable capacity as industrialization. As for computers and simulation, Liska has said:

21. Jozsef Bognar, "Overall Direction and Operation of the Economy," *The New
Hungarian Quarterly* (spring 1966).
22. Ibid., p. 8.   23. Ibid., p. 10.

Left unsaid, or even consciously denied, it became also more and more obvious in the course of the discussions that, even with electronic machines, it is impossible to centrally substitute the intricate information system of market price formation which expresses an infinite quantity of factors. Almost up to this day, even the boldest of such discussions urged only as much as an administrative pricing system that would imitate the market to a higher degree. The fact that if the best price from the point of economy is the one formed by the market, i.e., by free agreement, this makes a bureau created to imitate it obviously superfluous, has not even been hinted at.[24]

Neither has it been recognized that a result of decades of efforts at central planning has been to establish that for a modern economy there is no viable alternative to the market, whatever the efficiency of its signals. The goal of scientific socialism—the elimination of commodity production—is utopian.

The argument has been presented that central planning failed to establish itself organizationally and that the Soviet economy can be viewed as a polycentric system with signals that are irrational from the standpoint of economic efficiency. Instead of interpreting price and profit movements, the Soviet manager has interpreted "success indicators," and Soviet output has been largely a product of managerial interpretation of these signals. By focusing on the "gross output indicator," Soviet managers have been able to achieve the rewards of success even though their outputs have been poorly related to the needs of the users. In my account the major difference between the Soviet economy and a market economy lies in the rationality of the signals for managerial interpretation. I do not suggest that the Soviet system was designed to produce this difference but that it is an *ex post* result of efforts to eliminate commodity production. Looking at the Soviet economy from the standpoint of my polycentric model, the economic reforms are not, as is generally believed, a matter of radical organizational change but a matter of replacing signals that are less rational with signals that are more rational from the standpoint of economic efficiency.

If the Soviet Union has not a centrally planned economy, it cannot abandon central planning; what can be abandoned are efforts at central planning. These efforts at central planning have introduced

24. Liska, "The Development of Market Relations," p. 7.

non-market criteria into the role of market criteria. The result has been irrational signals for managerial interpretation, and the irrationality of production in the Soviet Union has been the consequence.

Figures 11 and 12 illustrate my theoretical classification of the Soviet economy. Each figure represents the set of all characteristics of economies. Any element or point is a single characteristic of some economy or economies. Any economy is one of two organizational types: (1) commodity production or production for sale (polycentric), represented in Figure 11 by a circle including points A and C, but not B; or (2) non-commodity production or production for direct use (ritual economies, centrally planned economies), represented in Figure 11 by a circle including points A and B, but not C. Both types are characterized by division of labor. Among the economies having intersecting sets of characteristics containing A and C are the U.S. and the U.S.S.R. (Figure 12), sharing in common a mode of production (i.e., basic economic organization), national policy making, similar elements of rationality (e.g., contracts) and irrationality (e.g., allowing individual productive units to treat waste

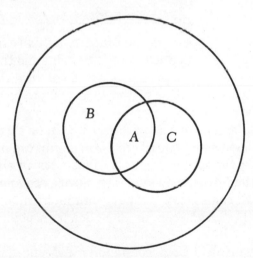

A—division of labor element
B—production for direct-use element
C—production for sale element

FIGURE 11.

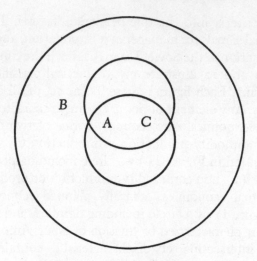

A—division of labor element
B—production for direct-use element
C—production for sale element

FIGURE 12.

disposal as costless), some private property rights (e.g., labor), and differing in the basic structure of property rights and the efficiency of signals for managerial interpretation. My theoretical classification of economic systems according to the mode of production that predominates is Marxian.

Based on the argument that in the Soviet Union there has been no capital market and no legal market in which firms can buy productive resources other than labor, Figure 13 illustrates an alternative classification of the Soviet economy. The Soviet economy has characteristics of both commodity and non-commodity modes, i.e., the set representing the Soviet economy includes both points C and B as well as A.

Acknowledgment of both commodity and non-commodity production in the Soviet Union is congruous with the official characterization given by Soviet ideological spokesmen. However, as Marx emphasized, although both modes may be found in all economies and are historically intersecting—i.e., peripheral trade may be found

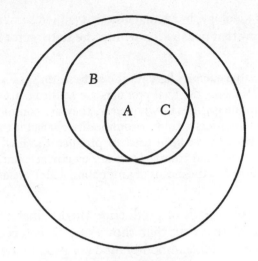

A—division of labor element
B—production for direct-use element
C—production for sale element

FIGURE 13.

in and between ritual economies in which production is organized
for direct use rather than for sale on the market, and some production for direct use is found in the U.S.—the predominant mode determines the classification.

It has been maintained in the Soviet Union that production
within the state sector for the state sector is not commodity production. The agricultural production of the collective farms and the production of consumer goods within the state sector have been
officially recognized as commodity production. However, in the
Soviet Union the state has found it necessary for a money payment
to accompany the passing of means of production from one unit to
another within the state sector. Lange has noted the difficulty in the
official position.[25] Lange terms the products produced within the
state sector "quasi-commodities." This is an effort on Lange's part to
introduce some honesty into the official position without completely

25. Oskar Lange, ed., *Problems of Political Economy of Socialism* (New Delhi:
People's Publishing House, 1962), p. 9.

contravening ideology, but Lange uses his coined term as a guise and goes on to show that production within the state sector is commodity production:

> The law of value operates here [in the state sector] indirectly by means of imputation. Since the final products are sold to consumers or to co-operatives, municipalities or whomever, they are commodities. By imputation this transfers a kind of commodity character to the means of production which have been used to produce the final commodities. The values of the final commodities are by any accounting process reflected backwards to the means of production which are used to produce them (p. 9).

The commodity mode of production predominates in the Soviet Union. No analysis exists that shows the Soviet economy to be characterized by a non-commodity mode of production. As the matter stands, the standard classification of the Soviet economy as a centrally planned one is based merely on the acceptance of a claim.

CHAPTER 5

Oskar Lange's Theory of Socialist Planning: An Obscurant of Socialist Aspirations

It is more than three decades since Lange published his famous paper that had instant success as a (long-awaited) theory of socialist planning.[1] Interest in the theory has recently revived as a result of awareness that economic reforms in the Soviet bloc constitute abandonment of efforts at central planning,[2] rather than reforms of planned systems. For Abram Bergson this raises "an issue long familiar in theory: the economic efficiency of market socialism."[3] This is a curious revival of the theory that was accepted as a refutation of Mises's objections to the theoretical possibility of socialist planning.[4] That it can be employed both as a system of socialist planning and as a system that results from the abandonment of planning in a socialist state indicates the role Lange's theory has played in obscuring the matter of socialist planning. If, as Bergson suggests, the direction of reforms in the Soviet Union is toward market socialism, this implies the frustration of aspirations that fired the Bolshevik Revolution.

1. Oskar Lange, "On the Economic Theory of Socialism," *Review of Economic Studies*, parts I-II, vol. IV (October 1936 and February 1937), pp. 53-71, 123-42. References in this chapter are to the reprinted form of Lange's paper in *On the Economic Theory of Socialism*, edited by B. E. Lippincott (Minneapolis: University of Minnesota Press, 1956).

2. See, for example, Abram Bergson, "Market Socialism Revisited," *Journal of Political Economy*, vol. 75, no. 5 (October 1967), pp. 655, 670.

3. Ibid., p. 655.

4. Ludwig von Mises, "Die Wirtschaftsrechnung im sozialistischen Gemeinwesen," *Archiv für Sozialwissenschaften*, vol. XLVII, April 1920), pp. 86-121. An English translation is in *Collectivist Economic Planning*, edited by F. A. Hayek (London: Routledge, 1935), pp. 87-130.

The analysis in this chapter shows why Drewnowski's assertion that the Lange-type model has nothing to do with socialist planning is correct.[5] This chapter also shows that the belief, which has been incorporated in the orthodoxy for three decades, that there is an alternative to the market for a modern economy is based on error and gives an analysis in the history of ideas to show how the error arose. The models of the so-called "socialist alternative" are only efforts at market simulation. The relevance of an analysis that purports to deal with socialism and central economic planning is called into question. Apparently that analysis has never acknowledged a matter basic to its use—and that is the question of what are its criteria for the theoretical classification of economic systems. If these criteria are not to be organizational criteria, how is an economy organized to produce "commodities" in keeping with principles of economic efficiency any different fundamentally whether it is organized by real-world markets or their simulation?

As I have shown, the program of Marxian socialism was one of transforming economic organization from a market system into a planned system of direct association in order to establish a new basis for relations between men. On this new basis a new society would arise. "The market itself will cease to exist,"[6] and man for the first time becomes "master of his own social organization"[7] and "with full consciousness, makes his own history."[8] This is the foundation of "planned economy."

Since it was this program of eliminating market relations toward which von Mises directed his criticism, a theory that empties socialist planning of socialist content and establishes socialism on the basis of exchange relations of the market is no answer to von Mises. Instead, by equating the achievement of competitive equilibrium with the goal of socialism, the Lange-type model takes the problem of socialist planning out of its historical context and obscures it.

5. Jan Drewnowski, "The Economic Theory of Socialism: A Suggestion for Reconsideration," Journal of Political Economy, vol. LXIX, no. 4 (August 1961), pp. 341-42.

6. Nikolai Bukharin, The Economics of the Transitional Period, cited from Adam Kaufman, "The Origin of the Political Economy of Socialism," Soviet Studies, vol. IV, no. 3 (January 1953), p. 245.

7. Frederick Engels, Anti-Dühring, 2nd ed. (Moscow: Foreign Languages Publishing House, 1959), p. 390.

8. Ibid., p. 391.

By transforming the objective of socialism into the issue of economic efficiency, economists created a socialism that no socialist ever believed in, placed hopes in, or fought for. This "socialism" has an extensive literature over its possibility[9] in spite of the fact that there has never been a socialist movement behind it.[10] The famous "socialist controversy" between Western economists is not about socialism but about the logical consistency of models of market simulation, their determinacy, stability, and convergence toward equilibrium. Within the context of this socialist controversy, the possibility of socialism depends on whether the market economy can be successfully simulated. This is why it has been a socialism interesting only to economic theoreticians.

The Logical Problem of the Lange Paradigm

The inappropriateness of the Lange model as a theory of socialist planning is not only demonstrated by its abandonment of the intentions of socialist planning but also by the logical impasse it presents for the theoretical classification of economic systems. The Lange model is constructed from economic theory that presupposes the exchange relationships of commodity production. Therefore, although the Lange model purports to establish the possibility of socialist planning, the model has the polycentric organizational structure of commodity production built in as a given of the economic theory out of which the model is constructed. By building a model of socialism on the categories of economic theory, Lange disregarded the hierarchical prerequisites of socialist organization.

The Lange-type model was the framework for the theoretic debate on the possibility of socialist planning that was waged during the in-

9. See, for example, Abram Bergson, "Socialist Economics" in *Survey of Contemporary Economics*, edited by Howard Ellis (Philadelphia: Blakiston, 1948), vol. I, pp. 412-48; and Benjamin N. Ward, *The Socialist Economy* (New York: Random House, 1967), pp. 14-40.

10. Recent economic reforms in Eastern Europe and the Soviet Union might be interpreted as constituting a socialist movement behind market socialism, but such a movement toward "commodity production" is in fact a movement away from socialism. See the Soviet economist A. Eremin, who, recognizing that "in the 'model of market socialism' the principal emphasis is on the need for the regeneration of commodity production," denies that socialism is "a species of commodity production" and strongly states that market socialism is "a definite anti-Marxist concept" ("On the Concept of 'Market Socialism,'" *Problems of Economics*, vol. XIII, no. 4, August 1970, pp. 3-20).

terwar period. Because the model takes as given the organizational relationships of the market, that is, the commodity mode of production, the debate was in terms of economic efficiency and convergence
toward equilibrium. The framework of the debate prevented the debate from penetrating the organizational basis necessary for a system
of socialist planning. The theoretical classification of economic systems depends on organizational criteria, that is, modes of production,
but the Lange paradigm precludes any organizational structure other
than that of commodity production and defines socialism in terms of
property rights.

The result is a logical inconsistency that allows a contradictory dual
status to the Lange model. For example, Bergson explicitly refers to
Lange's theory both as one of market organization of publicly owned
firms ("market socialism") in which the determination of inputs and
outputs is left to managers of production units[11] and also as "a planning scheme."[12] Later in his paper this contradictory dualism comes
together in the idea of a Central Planning Board (CPB) existing
simultaneously with the autonomy of managers.[13] This inconsistency
reflects the contradiction between the central planning vocabulary of
the Lange model and its market organizational structure. The contradictory dualism of the Lange model has been upheld by the willing-
ness to overlook the logical inconsistency in assigning it a dual status.
With this inconsistent duality, the Lange model was able to establish
the theoretical possibility of socialist planning on the basis of the
very market principles that socialist planning was supposed to replace.

This chapter will critique the Lange model on the grounds that it
is (1) organized as a market system in contradiction to the hierarchic
structure required for central economic planning, and (2) a system of
exchange relations embodying the very commodity production that
was to be eliminated by socialist planning. Lange's neglect of the
organizational requirements of central planning reduces the role of
his CPB to dressing the market in socialist vocabulary.

The Theory of Oskar Lange

In reply to von Mises who asserted in 1920 that "socialism is
the abolition of rational economy," Lange (among others) advanced

11. Abram Bergson, "Market Socialism Revisited," p. 656.
12. Ibid., p. 661.   13. Ibid., p. 665.

the theory that the central planning authority could achieve control over production by directing its subordinate managers to operate society's economic enterprises in accordance with the principles of competitive economic theory.[14] Lange never uses the term "market socialism." Throughout his analysis there is a CPB, and he explicitly views its actions as replacing market organization with a hierarchical structure of central planning.

Lange discusses central economic planning in two forms of socialist systems. One is completely centralized. In the other there is a "genuine market for consumers' goods and for the services of labor," but no market for capital goods and productive resources outside of labor (p. 73). In neither system are the managers of enterprises to be guided by profit maximization (p. 75). Instead, the CPB imposes rules on the managers that determine the combination of factors of production and the scale of output (p. 75). The rules can be put in the form of instructions "to use always the method of production (i.e., combination of factors) which minimizes average cost and to produce as much of each service or commodity as will equalize marginal cost and the price of the product" (p. 78).

In order for the managers of production to be able to follow these rules, "the prices of the factors and of the products must, of course, be given" (p. 78). Under the form of socialist planning in which there is "freedom of choice in consumption and freedom of choice of occupation" (p. 72), the prices of consumers' goods and services of labor are determined in a market (p. 78); "in all other cases they are fixed by the Central Planning Board" (p. 78). In Lange's theory, "those prices being given, the supply of products and the demand for factors are determined" (p. 78).

He recognizes that if the prices fixed by the CPB are arbitrary, they will have neither economic nor planning significance. His solution is for the CPB to impose the "parametric function of prices" on the managers as an accounting rule (p. 81). In Lange's mind this gives the CPB rational, central control over output. He writes that the fixed "prices alone are the variables determining the demand and supply of commodities" (pp. 69, 81).

His procedure of socialist planning then is one of tâtonnement—

14. Lange, "On the Economic Theory of Socialism."

a "method of trial and error based on the parametric function of prices" (p. 86). Constructing this system leads Lange to state:

> The Central Planning Board performs the function of the market. It establishes the rules for combining factors of production and choosing the scale of output of a plant, for determining the output of an industry, for the allocation of resources, and for the parametric use of prices in accounting. Finally, it fixes the prices so as to balance the quantity supplied and demanded of each commodity. It follows that a substitution of planning for the functions of the market is quite possible and workable" (pp. 82-83).

The Absence of Hierarchical Organization

It is clearly stated that the market is replaced by a process of planning. Lange further writes that "all decisions of the managers of production and of the productive resources in public ownership and also all decisions of individuals as consumers and as suppliers of labor are made on the basis of these prices" fixed by the CPB (p. 86).

However, the CPB is a redundant entity. The only prices fixed by it are the initial ones at the beginning of the procedure of *tâtonnement*, and, according to Lange, these "fixed" prices are the existing market-determined prices—"the prices *historically given*" (p. 86). All other prices are determined by demand and supply through a process of mutual adjustment devoid of central planning. Lange writes that "prices alone are the variables determining the demand and supply of commodities," but according to his own words the prices are not the right ones unless supply and demand are equal: "the determinateness of the accounting prices holds, however, only if all discrepancies between demand and supply of a commodity are met by an appropriate change of its price" (p. 93).

We are returned to the more familiar notion that it is supply and demand that determine price, rather than the other way round. And what determines supply and demand? In Lange's system it is the people in the market: "the preferences of consumers, as expressed by their demand prices, are the guiding criteria in production and in the allocation of resources" (pp. 72-73).

It is necessary to acknowledge that contrary to what Lange writes and even Hayek seems to accept,[15] these prices fixed by the CPB are not beyond the control of the market. If producers and consumers do not like them, the CPB has to change them, so that irrespective of whatever legal powers Lange gives the CPB over price and his insinuation that the CPB controls production by fixing prices, it is obvious that the only function of the CPB with regard to prices is to announce what has already happened in the market. If the individual managers are following the rules that Lange says they are to follow, the collective body of managers through their mutual interaction in purchasing factors, guided by consumer demands for final goods, are determining the levels and rates of outputs. The resources employed, the production functions used, the basket of final goods, and the relative prices of factors and final goods are all purely a result of the market process.

Lange describes an economy completely directed from a planning center, hierarchical to the nth degree:

> a socialist system where freedom of choice in consumption and freedom of choice of occupation are nonexistent and where the allocation of resources, instead of being directed by the preferences of consumers, is directed by the aims and valuations of the bureaucracy in charge of the administration of the economic system. In such a system the Central Planning Board decides which commodities are to be produced and in what quantities, the consumers' goods produced being distributed to the citizens by rationing and the various occupations being filled by assignment. In such a system also rational economic accounting is possible, only that the accounting reflects the preferences of the bureaucrats in the Central Planning Board, instead of those of the consumers. The Central Planning Board has to fix a scale of preferences which serves as the basis of valuation of consumers' goods (pp. 90-91).

Lange says that his rules and the procedure of trial and error are applicable also to this totally planned economy. However, rules taken from a market economy and which reflect its structure can have no applicability to a centrally planned economy. To give such rules organizational meaning in a planned system, as does Lange, is to override the intended hierarchic structure. It is a denial of a planned

15. F. A. Hayek, "Socialist Calculation: The Competitive 'Solution,'" *Economica*, New Series, vol. VII (May 1940), pp. 125-49.

economy to have individual producers following these rules since, if they are, then *they* are determining the levels and rates of outputs, and the hierarchical economic structure of the system evaporates. The CPB has its functions taken over by the market. Here is a clear example of a leading advocate of central planning grossly confusing the administrative natures of a planned system and a market economy.

In a planned economy the managers of plants can make no decision about the allocation of resources and the rates and levels of outputs as they would be if they followed Lange's rules. The decision as to the combination of factors "that minimize the average cost of production" must be made by the CPB when it decides "which commodities are to be produced and in what quantities" and handed down to the plant managers in the form of orders or instructions. The CPB cannot determine prices independently of the levels and rates of output.

The Non-applicability of the Marginal Rule[16]

Under the Lange-type formulation, the element of conscious central control is absent; it is present only in words. In competitive theory the equating of marginal cost to price is the result of wealth-maximizing behavior; no one has as his conscious purpose to make marginal cost equal to price. However, under Lange's formulation of a planned economy, a result of competitive theory becomes the principle of administrative control. It becomes the task of the subordinate managers, the test of their success, and the criterion for their reward.

I have argued that Lange's theory is rooted in market organization of the economy in contradiction to the hierarchic requirements of central planning. Lange overlooked the organizational character of the model from which he borrowed the "marginal rule," and he

16. In different terms and from a different direction, James M. Buchanan arrives at the point made in this section in *Cost and Choice* (Chicago: Markham, 1969). The point is similar to that of G. F. Thirlby in "The Ruler," *South African Journal of Economics,* vol. XIV (December 1946), pp. 253-76; and Jack Wiseman, "Uncertainty, Costs, and Collectivist Economic Planning," *Economica,* vol. XX (May 1953), pp. 118-28. I derive the point from organizational, not cost, considerations.

likewise overlooked the purely formalistic character of his own theory, which dealt with equating marginal properties without regard to the organizational system involved. He believed that his planning authority had in the marginal rule a method of subordinating economic activity to its directive control. But this effort to make an application to central planning of what is only an illustrative principle (that throws light on the kind of coordination achieved in the economic utilization of resources by a market economy) forces all judgment concerning the organization of production on the individual managers. I will now argue that the marginal rule, on which the Lange model depends, is not applicable as a *formal directive* even in a market economy.

Under real-world conditions characterized by the passage of time, the marginal rule gives no clear guidance to those directed to organize production in accordance with it. Introducing the element of time brings in uncertainty and requires the exercise of judgment. Neither uncertainty nor judgment is present in the formulation of perfect competition from which Lange took his idea of the marginal rule.

Although the elimination of uncertainty by central planning was a leading attraction to many adherents, it is present in Lange's system which is based on "the procedure of trial and error." It might appear that the "fixing" of prices by the CPB would give the objectively known data for equating marginal cost to price. However, the managers cannot avoid knowing that the prices in this *tâtonnement* process are merely of temporary validity, and they will base their actions on anticipations of the direction of change.[17]

Because uncertainty is unavoidable whether in Lange's system or in a real-world market with resources publicly or privately owned, managerial behavior cannot amount to adaption to known conditions. The manager's task is to decide between alternative resource allocations on the basis of estimates of future conditions. Thus, excess of

17. It might be thought to eliminate the organizing initiative of managers by prohibiting any economic undertakings until the right marginal-cost-price relationships are found for all products. This might seem to turn the managers into mathematical computing agents of the central authority—a system of explicit calculation that Lange's system was designed to avoid. However, each single manager still calculates his own adjustment with respect to all others, and optimality is a *result* of the individual computations; the "plan" is a historical result of the simulated market process.

total revenue over total cost may result from successful prediction as
well as from "non-optimal" organization of production. This renders
the marginal rule directive inappropriate as the criterion of managerial success.

Since the problem actually faced by managers is one of choosing
among alternative lines of action on the basis of estimates, it is a
matter of personal judgment—a skillful process of tacit integration
that can be formalized only in theory. A manager cannot undertake
simultaneously all his alternative courses of action. The alternative
chosen depends on his judgment of the outcomes of the possible
lines of action. A marginal rule directive could only check the ability
of a manager to forecast the outcome of the alternative he chooses
(in the sense of it being profitable or not) and control the rate of
output; it cannot check its relative profitability against the alternatives that were not followed. Therefore, a marginal rule directive does
not set a manager's task because it does not determine whether he
should have chosen the course of action that he chose.

The point is not that there is a formal difference in economic
theory between the marginal rule and profit maximization. Market
organization could not be dressed in the clothes of hierarchy if the
directive to managers is to maximize profits. However, the notion of
a central planning board imposing the marginal rule upon managers
of production units evidently sufficed to convince economists that
the actions of individual managers could be directed by the CPB,
which could plan economic activity by means of such control. Economists should be derided, perhaps, for their lack of perception, but
we have simply argued that no application of the marginal rule as a
formal directive is possible.

Sources of the Langesque Illusion of Planning

A source of the planning illusion is Lange's separation of interdependent variables that are only formally distinguishable. Such
distinctions do not literally reflect reality. For explanation of an
autonomous system this is not serious if it is kept in mind that the
validity of the theory is formal and that its bearing on reality is illustrative. However, for theories that are to be used to reconstruct real-

ity, formal validity does not suffice. Lange gives a description of dialectical relationships in linear terms (as is often done in the classroom) and confuses his linear description with reality (which is mutually determining). He has a notion of making an application of his linear description to control economic activity. This error reinforces in his mind the illusion of the CPB directing production. Lange goes through the procedure of A determining B, B determining C, and so on, and comes to the conclusion that the prices fixed by the CPB are the sole variables and that they determine supply and demand (p. 81).

Certainly the perpetuation of the illusion is indebted to Hayek's critique[18] which accepted the Lange-type proposals on their own terms and thereby gave them an undeserved credibility. If the arch-critic accepts such proposals as systems of socialist planning and proceeds to discuss the problems of the systems, what could give greater guarantee of the success of the proposals? By focusing his critique on the comparative inefficiency of the Lange-type system as an equilibrating mechanism, Hayek allowed the fact to be obscured that the function of a CPB lies in the determination of the plan that replaces market relationships. As a consequence, the meaning of socialist planning was lost in the succeeding literature, and commodity production has since been represented in the literature as "socialist planning."

Barone's article[19] is a definite foundation of the illusion. Although Barone might have meant his article to be a refutation of the possibility of socialist planning, it allowed an interpretation that falsified the problem in two ways.

First, acknowledging the intentions of socialism, Barone seems to deny need for money or prices in his model of a socialist economy (p. 267). Instead there are "equivalents," a semantic distinction that veils the illusion in the manner often used since. Lange calls them "accounting prices" and Leontief calls them "fictitious accounting

18. Hayek, "Socialist Calculation: The Competitive 'Solution.'"
19. Enrico Barone, "Il ministro della produzione nello stato collecttivista," *Giornale degli Economisti e Rivista di Statistica*, vol. XXXVII (September and October 1908), pp. 267-93, 391-414. Reference is to the English translation in Hayek, *Collectivist Economic Planning*, pp. 245-90.

prices."[20] Although Barone's semantics have led many economists astray, he did not fool himself. A few pages later Barone writes that an "equivalent" is "the price, under another name" (p. 272).

Second, Barone writes that he proposes "to determine in what manner the Ministry concerned with production ought to direct it" (p. 246)—implying concern with the organizational structure of a centrally planned economy—but what he accomplishes is to formalize in mathematical terms the operation of economic theory in exhausting the product in an autonomous system. Often since, mathematical expositions of economic theory have been confused with central planning.[21] In the August 1961 *Journal of Political Economy*, Drewnowski calls mathematical formulation of market-generated criteria "the centralized decisions approach" to economic planning (p. 342).[22]

Finally, von Mises's formulation of his argument is itself ultimately responsible for the confusion. Whatever his familiarity with the intellectual foundations of socialist intentions, he was faced with a program of action that was fantastic in its lack of foundation. When, for example, Engels wrote that under socialism "people will be able to manage everything very simply, without the intervention

20. In his review in the June 1938 *American Economic Review* of Pigou's *Socialism versus Capitalism*, Wassily Leontief writes: "With great precision and clarity Professor Pigou describes the structure and operation of the hypothetical price system in a socialist economy. (The theoretical possibility of such a system, Professor Mises' objections notwithstanding, can be considered by now to be definitely established.) Following the path indicated by Lange and other authors, he visualizes it as a system of fictitious accounting prices and interest rates" (p. 411).

If prices, whether generated by markets or the simulation of markets, guide the allocation of resources, they are real; and it is illogical to refer to them as fictitious. The curious terminology used and accepted by such distinguished economists underlines the fact that during the 1930s it was still tacitly recognized that socialist planning and market pricing were antithetical. Therefore, it was necessary to deny the existence of market pricing in the models of socialism by terming the prices, on which the models relied, fictitious. This is the use of artificial abstraction to make a model appear other than what it is. The obscuration was not the result of conscious intention but of superficial familiarity with socialist aspirations.

21. Market simulation is also confused with central planning. It has evidently not occurred to numerous writers that a simulation of a system must reflect the structure of that system. A simulation of the market reflects the structure of the market and the exchange relationships of "commodity production."

22. Since a theory of socialist planning does not exist, the failure of even such a theory to ensure perfection cannot be demonstrated by the eager analysis of our anatomists (reference is to F. Bator, "The Anatomy of Market Failure," *Quarterly Journal of Economics*, August 1958, pp. 351-79). In this way socialism is protected.

of much-vaunted 'value' "[23] and Bukharin wrote that "as soon as we deal with an organized national economy, all the basic 'problems' of political economy, such as price, value, profit, etc., simply disappear"[24]—they were serious.

Von Mises was passionate in his refutation of this socialist program. Simultaneously, he defended the concept of private property. By joining his arguments he structured the problem such that to those who later joined in the debate (particularly if they were unfamiliar with, or not serious about, the socialist intention to eliminate commodity production), the possibility of socialist planning could appear to turn on whether there could be rational economic criteria in the absence of a private capital market. From that time forward the definition of socialism was cut loose from the qualities that had given it historical force.

The New School of Socialist Thought

Dickinson,[25] Durbin,[26] Lange, and Lerner[27] were preceded in the structure of their thought by Taylor[28] and Barone. However, in addition to pursuing the same ideas in the same period of time, the former four attributed positive values to socialism and can be regarded as leading members of a new school of socialist thought. A distinctive characteristic of this school of thought is that its members were critical of the real-world market economy not because it reflected the organizational structure of commodity production but because it does not live up to the illustrative theory of pure competition! Their critique of the market is not founded on the basis of a true socialist estrangement from the market that fired an intention to replace one system of organization, X, with a totally different system

23. Engels, Anti-Dühring (Foreign Languages Publishing House), p. 427.

24. Cited from Kaufman, "Origin of the Political Economy of Socialism," p. 245.

25. H. D. Dickinson, "Price Formation in a Socialist Community," Economic Journal, vol. XLIII (June 1933), pp. 237-50 and Economics of Socialism (London: Oxford University Press, 1939).

26. E. F. M. Durbin, "Economic Calculus in a Planned Economy," Economic Journal, vol. XLVI (December 1936), pp. 676-90.

27. A. P. Lerner, "Economic Theory and Socialist Economy," Review of Economic Studies, vol. II (October 1934), pp. 51-61.

28. Fred M. Taylor, "The Guidance of Production in a Socialist State," American Economic Review, vol. 19, no. 1 (March 1929).

of organization, Y, but is a critique characterized by the intellectual phenomenon of preferring the model X to the literal X. They desired what they called socialism in order to achieve the efficiency of the competitive model. Dickinson explicitly equates the achievement of competitive equilibrium with the goal of socialism: "The beautiful systems of economic equilibrium described by Bohm-Bawerk, Wieser, Marshall and Cassel are not descriptions of society as it is but prophetic visions of a socialist economy of the future."[29]

Since the concern of Dickinson, Durbin, Lange, and Lerner was with economic efficiency, full employment, and the distribution of income, they never penetrated the organizational requirements of central planning. Therefore, they never had cause to notice the contradiction inherent in their models. Unlike revolutionary socialists, they accepted the organizational structure of commodity production, and their critique of the market was mainly in terms of the standards of economic theory, standards which socialism had rejected. Although later in life Lange was familiar with the Marxian analysis of commodity production,[30] there is no evidence that the new socialists were familiar with the fundamental Marxian critique of market organization at the time they developed their models of socialist planning, and there is clear evidence that even later in life Dickinson had an erroneous understanding of what Marx meant by commodity production.[31] However, they were aware of a historical connection between socialism and planning and had the concept of a central planning board in their models even though it was in contradiction to the implicit organizational structure of the models.

29. H. D. Dickinson, "Price Formation in a Socialist Community," p. 247.
30. Oskar Lange, *Problems of Political Economy of Socialism* (New Delhi: Peoples Publishing House, 1962).
31. In *Economic Problems in a Free Society*, a revised transcript of the addresses delivered at a refresher course for tutors published by the Central Joint Advisory Committee on Tutorial Classes, London, 1948, Dickinson writes: "There are fundamentally two ways of organizing the work of a more or less free community—through the wages system, or through what Marx called 'commodity production.' We are accustomed to a society in which the great majority of people are doing a job for a wage or salary. . . . But it is not the only way of arranging things. There is also the system under which people, instead of selling their labour power to an employer or public body, embody their labour power in a commodity, which they then sell, either directly to the consumer or to a merchant. In its one case you have the choice of a job at a wage or salary, and in the other case you have what might be called the choice of a trade" (p. 13). With such a misrepresentation of the meaning of commodity production to tutors, it is no wonder that the socialist heritage has been lost.

The new school of socialist thought was opposed on organizational grounds not by Hayek and other critics of socialism but by representatives of the original socialist intentions. For example, in his critique Dobb writes: "Either planning means over-riding the autonomy of separate decisions or it apparently means nothing at all."[32] In a review of Dobb's book, Rogin writes: "In the closing chapter on 'Economic Law in a Socialist Economy,' the author states that despite its recent modifications with respect to monopoly, contemporary economic theory will play a negligible role in a socialist economy. It cannot be otherwise with a theory which premises the allocation of resources on the autonomous decisions of entrepreneurs."[33]

Dobb recognized intuitively what the argument of this chapter demonstrates: (1) the purpose of the socialism that was a historical force was the replacement of market relationships by central planning rather than the achievement of a competitive equilibrium (given a growth rate and income distribution); and (2) the Lange-type model is merely a model of publicly owned firms operating according to market principles that socialism intended to abolish.

The outcome of the socialist controversy has not been to prove the possibility of socialist planning, as is believed, but to vindicate market relationships. This vindication in theory apparently is reinforced in practice by the outcome of the "Soviet experiment."

The most far-reaching result of the socialist controversy is unrelated to socialism and is the critique of the real-world market economy from the standpoint of the standards of a theory whose bearing on reality is merely illustrative. Although man has ability to improve his social and economic organization, and the desire to do so is legitimate, much market criticism can be compared to criticizing inanimate matter for not reflecting the theories of physics and chemistry. There is a questionable normative element in a science that criticizes reality on the basis of theoretical standards. Much market inefficiency is purely formalistic in character. Breast-beating in the real world over market inefficiency, the validity of which is merely formal, is illogical; it certainly is not socialism.

32. Maurice Dobb, *Political Economy and Capitalism*, rev. ed. (New York: International Publishers, 1940), p. 276.

33. Leo Rogin, *American Economic Review*, vol. XXVIII, no. 2 (June 1938), p. 329.

CHAPTER 6

Speculative Excess as a Force in History

The resolution of the Central Committee of the Hungarian Socialist Workers' Party of May 7, 1966, which according to Balassa is the basic document introducing the economic reform in Hungary, states:

> The development of an active role for the market requires that the laborious and bureaucratic system of the centralized allocation of materials and products . . . should give place to commercial relations, i.e., producers should be able to decide, within their range of activities, what and how much they produce and offer for sale, as well as in what quantity and from whom they purchase the necessary inputs . . . producers and users should be free to establish commercial or co-operative relationships—sellers and buyers should be free to agree on the conditions of sale and, within the limits of government price determination, also on the prices; the buyers should be free to choose, within the limits dictated by the national interest, between domestic goods and imports, and the sellers between selling on domestic or on export markets.[1]

Balassa states that the official institution of a market system in Hungary is accompanied by profitability becoming "the sole measure of the firm's success, as well as the source of incentive payments and of funds for new investments."[2] Although all Soviet-type economies have not yet officially acknowledged their polycentric structures and taken steps to reintroduce the normal market signals, many observers

1. Cited by Bela Balassa in "The Economic Reform in Hungary," *Economica,* New Series, vol. XXXVII, no. 145 (February 1970), p. 4.
2. Ibid.

have noted that the Hungarian direction is the direction of them all. The outcome of the fierce socialist efforts, often sustained beyond the point of humane considerations, to eliminate commodity production and institute "planned production for community consumption" is the vindication of the market.

How have scholars explained this reconciliation between socialists and what they hated most—market organization? Prevalent opinion explains the reconciliation by explaining away the purpose of the revolution and by denying that the ideas behind it have had any effect on the Soviet-type economies. Planning is said to have been so successful in creating a complex industrialized economy that it has pushed itself out of the picture; it has created an informational problem and can no longer cope with the situation. The result of prevalent opinion is to cover the failure of the revolutionary intentions by redefining the goal of socialism as equal to its *ex post* results, which are divergent from its *ex ante* intentions. Thus, scholarship has been effective in producing interpretations that provide historical justifications for every turn of Soviet events and in blinding the world to the important role played by folly in Soviet experience.

The analysis in this book offers a different approach. I have viewed Soviet economic history as a product of the interaction of utopian intentions with a refractory reality, an interaction that has ended in the abandonment of the original aims. In my account, economic and historical necessities have to make room for speculative excess as a force in history.

According to Marx, the evils of capitalism are due to its commodity character. This basic Marxian theme is developed in Chapter 1, which offers an interpretation of Marxian alienation that shows the consistency of Marx's general scheme and the programmatic implications of his work. Chapter 2 shows the application of the Marxian program to the Soviet economy and its failure, a failure that has not been generally acknowledged. Chapter 3 relates Marx's analysis of economic systems to organizational theory. The hierarchic structure of central planning is contrasted with the polycentric structure of production for sale on the market, to which Marx attributed all the ills of capitalism and the alienation of man. By differentiating between the organizational structure of the market and the rules and signals that condition its performance, market organization is established on the basis of theoretical principles that are more general than the ones that have traditionally provided its foundation.

Chapter 4 explains the Soviet economy as a polycentric organizational system that produces "commodities" and in which managers organize production by interpreting signals other than price and profit movements. The institution of material supply, the absence of a legal market for industrial materials, and the substitution of other signals for price and profit signals are seen as the result of unsuccessful efforts to establish a non-commodity mode of production. Thus, the Soviet economy is explained both in terms of organizational principles and Marxian aspirations. Central planning failed to establish itself organizationally, but the attempt to plan the economy accounts for the peculiar characteristics of the Soviet economic system. Chapter 5 shows why the Western debate over the possibility of socialist planning is a failure and how the debate contributed to the obscuration of the aspirations of socialism and, thereby, Soviet history, and generated a new normative critique of the market.

What are the implications of this analysis? Many implications may be beyond the reach of my imagination and may only be seen by others. Many may find the implications of my emphasis on speculative excess as a force in Soviet history unthinkable, but the emphasis definitely suggests reformulations to historians. Also, the emphasis suggests that the origin in foundations of Western intellectual thought of recurrent utopian programmatic aspirations and denunciations must be identified.[3] Apparently, there is a contradiction in our intellectual foundations that produces in people of a certain sensitivity a disaffection from society that is effective in destroying cultures but not in attaining its aims; therefore, its result is to reincorporate into a social system the very elements that the disaffection seizes upon. This implies a future history of destruction, gradual rebuilding, and destruction that has definite implications for the idea of human progress, unless the problem in our intellectual foundations is identified and resolved.

The above are grand implications. Lesser implications are also

3. Michael Polanyi locates the problem in the contradiction between the demand for the moral perfection of society and scepticism of morality. See Polanyi, "On the Modern Mind," *Encounter* (May 1965) and "Beyond Nihilism" in *Knowing and Being: Essays by Michael Polanyi*, edited by Marjorie Grene (Chicago: University of Chicago Press, 1969).

interesting. If we define capitalism organizationally as did Marx, Bukharin, and Lenin, then the Soviet economy is capitalist. This raises questions about social ownership as a meaningful classificatory criterion. The Yugoslav economist Aleksander Bajt has recently argued that a distinction must be made between property in the real or economic sense and property in the purely juridical or legal sense. Bajt follows Marx in arguing that it is the economic or real sense that is meaningful as opposed to a legal sense which might only be a veil to hide the lack of true socialization.[4] He argues that economic efficiency requires property to be effective in its economic sense: "one cannot negate the economic necessity that entrepreneurs be proprietors of their products."[5] This, however, does not mean that legal forms are not economically important. The legal structure must allow property to be effective in its economic sense:

> If one wants to develop entrepreneurial activity in socialist enterprises, one has to provide enterprises with adequate legal rights in order to ex-change factors and products in as free a manner as possible. We avoid the term property rights in this connection and try to substitute some less embarrassing term, such as, for instance, "rights of utilization and administration," for it. However, once you take the independence of enterprises and their entrepreneurial activity, be they individual or col-lective, seriously, as we do in Yugoslavia, it always comes to the situation that enterprises do behave, and the legal structure has to enable them to behave, as if they were owners of the means of production which they use. I would not be surprised, therefore, if somewhere in the future this will find its expression in giving enterprises property rights in their means of production (property in the legal sense).[6]

Thus, with Bajt's analysis even the simulacrums of socialism vanish. Michael Polanyi has written that

> the Russian Revolution, that had conquered power in order to achieve a radically distinct form of economic organization that would be far more productive and also morally superior to commercial management,

4. Bajt does not define socialization in terms of a non-commodity mode of produc-tion. Following the path indicated by Lenin, he defines socialism in terms of what is attainable and probably means by it a "fair" distribution of income that does not inter-fere significantly with efficiency and productivity (measured by utility).

5. Aleksander Bajt, "Property in Capital and in the Means of Production in Social-ist Economies," The Journal of Law and Economics, vol. XI (April 1968), p. 3.

6. Ibid., p. 4.

has now demonstrated the fact there is no such possibility. By the time its fiftieth anniversary is celebrated, the Revolution may be widely recognized by its very successors as having been virtually pointless. It may live on henceforth in its emblems, in the way the Mexican Revolution has lived on without making much difference in substance.[7]

Once it is realized that socialist symbols are expressions of passion for conviviality and represent not experience but inordinate aspirations, perhaps men will stop allowing themselves to be used and absorbed by symbols and, instead, will use symbols as tools to understand reality. When men cease to be the victims of socialist symbolism, objectivity will return. Scholarship will again be set on the path of the truth, and history will cease being shaped by aims that do not bear on reality.

7. Michael Polanyi, "The Message of the Hungarian Revolution," *The American Scholar*, vol. 35 (autumn 1966), p. 675.

A Critique of Other Interpretations of Marxian Alienation

To put our interpretation of Marxian alienation into perspective, it is useful to consider other interpretations. Although several scholars have identified alienation as lying behind Marx's discussion of commodity fetishism, they have failed to see that alienation is merely a result of the more general phenomenon of commodity production and that it is manifested in all of the contradictions inherent in the commodity mode of production. This failure has led contemporary scholars to seek the source of Marxian alienation in a variety of things. For example, the cause of alienation has been located in the system of private ownership of property, the division of labor, and greed or money worship. All of these explanations are inadequate.

According to Daniel Bell, the alienation of man for Marx is in the property system.[1] Bell delineates two aspects of alienation: "men lost control over the conditions of work, and men lost the product of the labor."[2] Loss of control of work is caused by the division of labor and results in dehumanization. Loss of the product is caused by private ownership of the means of production and results in exploitation. Thus, dehumanization and exploitation appear as the two characteristics of alienation.

From Bell's analysis, it follows that to abolish alienation, it is necessary to abolish both the division of labor and private property. Bell states that under communism the division of labor will be eliminated when man

1. Daniel Bell, "The Debate on Alienation" in *Revisionism: Essays on the History of Marxist Ideas*, edited by Leopold Labedz (New York: Praeger, 1962), p. 200.
2. Ibid., pp. 203-04.

engages in a variety of work to develop his aptitudes and that private property will be eliminated by socialization.[3]

Bell's interpretation misplaces the basis and cause of alienation. From a correct insight in which he says that for Marx alienation was rooted in the organization of work, the study of which was central to *Capital*, Bell proceeds to locate the source of alienation in private property and the division of labor, neither of which is unique to capitalism.

Doubts concerning the relationship between private property and alienation should be dispelled by Marx's own words:

> Through *estranged, alienated labor*, then, the worker produces the relationship to this labor of a man alien to labor and standing outside it. The relationship of the worker to labor creates the relation to it of the capitalist (or whatever one chooses to call the master of labor). *Private property* is thus the product, the result, the necessary consequence, of *alienated labor*, of the external relation of the worker to nature and to himself.
>
> *Private* property thus results by analysis from the concept of *alienated labor*, i.e., of *alienated man*, of estranged labor, of estranged life, of *estranged* man.
>
> True, it is as a result of the *movement of private property* that we have obtained the concept of *alienated labor (of alienated life)* from political economy. But on analysis of this concept it becomes clear that though private property appears to be the source, the cause of alienated labor, it is rather its consequence, just as the gods are *originally* not the cause but the effect of man's intellectual confusion. Later this relationship becomes reciprocal.[4]

Both Marx and Engels make it clear that changes in class and property relations are results of the extension of commodity production. For example, during 1857-58, Marx wrote: "We may see that the development of exchange and exchange-value brings about the dissolution of labour's relations of property in its conditions of existence. . . . Production based on exchange-value and a community based on the exchange of these exchange-values . . . presuppose and produce the separation of labour from its objective conditions."[5]

3. Ibid., pp. 204-05.
4. Karl Marx, *The Economic and Philosophic Manuscripts of 1844* (New York: International Publishers, 1969), pp. 116-17.
5. Karl Marx, *Pre-Capitalist Economic Formations* (New York: International Publishers, 1965), pp. 113-14. Cf. Engels, *Anti-Dühring*.

It is the commodity form of production that dissolves the community into a mass of private producers. In Marx, therefore, capitalist property relations, which many have interpreted as the cause of alienation and exploitation, are a mere consequence of commodity production. Marx says that "according to the conditions of production, property will take different forms."[6] Marx views private property as the appropriate property form in a system of commodity production.[7] Since alienated labor is labor that produces commodities (and is itself a commodity), it follows that "wages are a direct consequence of estranged labor, and estranged labor is the direct cause of private property."[8] Therefore, private property cannot be eliminated unless the labor that produces commodities is eliminated. Marx criticizes Proudhon for failure to realize this and states that "*wages and private property are identical.*" Therefore:

> An *enforced increase of wages* . . . would therefore be nothing but *better payment for the slave*, and would not win either for the worker or for labor their human status and dignity.
>
> Indeed, even the *equality of wages* demanded by Proudhon only transforms the relationship of the present-day worker to his labor into the relationship of all men to labor. Society is then conceived as an abstract capitalist.[9]

Division of labor is a necessary but not a sufficient condition for commodity production. Marx writes:

> In the totality of different kinds of use-values or commodities, there is embodied a totality of equally diversified forms of useful labour. The kinds of useful labour can be divided into genera, species, subspecies, and varieties—for there is a social division of labour. This division of labour is essential to the production of commodities; although it is not true, conversely, that there is no social division of labour in the absence of commodity production. In the primitive communities of India there is social division of labour, but the products of this community production do not become commodities. To take an example that lies nearer to our hand, in every factory there is a systematic division of labour, but this division of labour is not brought into being by an exchange of individual products among the workers in the factory. The only products

6. Ibid., p. 95.
7. The Yugoslav economist Aleksander Bajt has recently expressed this view. See Chapter 6.
8. Marx, *Economic and Philosophic Manuscripts*, p. 118.
9. Ibid., pp. 117-18.

which confront one another as commodities are those produced by reciprocally independent enterprises.[10]

We know of no circumstance in human history when division of labor was not a feature of society. There is division of labor within self-sufficient family production or within the hierarchy of a factory without market exchange. In communism, Marx saw the end of commodity production— the end of market relations between mutually independent producers— and the inception of man's producing directly for society. Division of labor remains, though its deleterious effects would be mitigated by social regulation of production making it possible for a man to work in one capacity today and in another tomorrow.[11] The important difference is that labor and the products of labor no longer are commodities.

Neither is exploitation unique to capitalism. Both private property and

10. Karl Marx, *Capital*, vol. I (Everyman's Library; London: J. M. Dent, 1957), p. 11.

11. Excerpts from the following quotation from Karl Marx in *The German Ideology* (New York: International Publishers, 1968) are often used by those who argue that the division of labor is the source of Marxian alienation.

Further, the division of labor implies the contradiction between the interest of the separate individual or the individual family and the communal interest of all individuals who have intercourse with one another. And indeed, this communal interest does not exist merely in the imagination, as the "general good" but first of all in reality, as the mutual interdependence of the individuals among whom the labour is divided. And finally, the division of labour offers us the first example of how, as long as man remains in natural society, that is as long as a cleavage exists between the particular and the common interest, as long therefore as activity is not voluntarily, but naturally, divided, man's own deed becomes an alien power opposed to him, which enslaves him instead of being controlled by him. For as soon as labour is distributed, each man has a particular, exclusive sphere of activity, which is forced upon him and from which he cannot escape. He is a hunter, a fisherman, a shepherd, or a critical critic, and must remain so if he does not want to lose his means of livelihood; while in communist society, where nobody has one exclusive sphere of activity but each can become accomplished in any branch he wishes, society regulates the general production and thus makes it possible for me to do one thing today and another tomorrow, to hunt in the morning, fish in the afternoon, rear cattle in the evening, criticize after dinner, just as I have a mind, without ever becoming hunter, fisherman, shepherd or critic (p. 22).

What Marx is saying here is that a division of labor *established by market exchange* results in a cleavage between the particular and the common interest and in man's own deed becoming "an alien power opposed to him, which enslaves him instead of being controlled by him." Both the cleavage between the particular and common interest and the enslaving of man by his own economic activity cease in communist society which "regulates the general production" and establishes conscious social control over the division of labor.

By "natural society" Marx means in this instance market society. He uses the term "natural society" to equate technological man's blind existence in the market system with primitive man's blind existence in nature. Neither modern technological man nor primitive man has control over his economic existence. One is subservient to forces of exploitation can exist without there being alienated labor. The feudal lord owned the manor and exploited the serfs (whose labor obligations prevented them from having control over the conditions of work and the product of their labor)—but, as Marx points out, the obligations of the serf were met by payment of goods and services in kind, and commodities as such did not exist.[12] He writes that personal dependence forms the groundwork of feudal society and that in such a society "there is no necessity for labor and its products to assume a fantastic form different from their reality. They take the shape, in the transactions of society, of services in kind and payments in kind. Here the particular and natural form of labor, and not, as in a society based on production of commodities, its general abstract form, is the immediate social form of labor."[13] He goes on to say that "no matter, then, what we may think of the parts played by the different classes of people themselves in feudal society, the social relations between individuals in the performance of their labor appear at all events as their own mutual personal relations, and are not disguised under the shape of social relations between the products of labor."[14] He says that an example of directly associated labor is "close at hand in the patriarchal industries of a peasant family that produces corn, cattle, yarn, linen, and clothing for home use. These different articles are, as regards the family, so many products of its labor, but as between themselves, they are not commodities."[15]

By treating the exploitation of workers by capitalists as the cause of alienation, there is the implication that the worker is alienated whereas the capitalist is not. Marx points out that the capitalist is also dominated by the impersonal forces of the market: "competition makes the immanent laws of capitalist production to be felt by each individual capitalist as external coercive laws."[16]

nature, the other to forces of the market. When Marx refers to economic activity as voluntarily divided, he means men have united and established conscious social control over the economy in which they act only as they choose and are not pushed around by market forces.

12. Marx, *Capital*, vol. I (Everyman's Library), pp. 50-51.

13. Karl Marx, *Capital*, vol. I (Modern Library; New York: Random House, 1906), p. 89.

14. Ibid.   15. Ibid.

16. Ibid., p. 649. In *The Economic and Philosophic Manuscripts of 1844*, Marx emphasizes that it is not emancipation of the workers alone that is at stake but that "the emancipation of the workers contains universal human emancipation—and it contains this because the whole of human servitude is involved in the relation of the worker to production, and every relation of servitude is but a modification and consequence of this relation" (p. 118).

Socialization of the means of production is merely a means to an end. It makes possible central control over productive resources in order that central economic planning can replace the exchange relationships of the market. Marx sees "jointly owned means of production" in conjunction with "a definite social plan."[17] Engels lends support to this interpretation. Alienation is abolished "when society, by taking possession of all means of production and *using them on a planned basis*, has freed itself and all its members from the bondage in which they are at present held by these means of production which they themselves have produced but which now confront them as irresistible, extraneous force."[18]

Commodity production reaches its apogee in capitalism, and the uniqueness of capitalism lies in commodity production as the dominant mode of production. Although division of labor and private property are aspects of capitalism, they are not unique to capitalism and do not define it as a mode of production. The *differentia specifica* of commodity production is production for exchange by mutually independent producers. A communist mode of production is brought about by conscious social organization of production for the direct use of the community and not for sale on the market. Many recognize that Marx thought that alienation would be abolished by communism, but they have failed to see in what way communism differs fundamentally from capitalism as a mode of production.

We have argued that neither of the objective phenomena—private property and the division of labor—is the source of Marxian alienation. Now we shall analyze the argument that the subjective phenomenon, greed, is the source of Marxian alienation and simultaneously attempt to resolve the controversy over the relationship of the concept of alienation to the mature Marx's work.

With regard to existing controversy, our position is clear. We disagree with Hook who maintains that "the section on the fetishism of commodities in *Capital* has no connection except literary flavoring with the metaphysical tripe in the unpublished early manuscripts."[19] We are sympathetic to the idea of others that alienation is a central theme of Marx and that the thread that holds together Marx's system is the concept of a

17. Marx, *Capital*, vol. I (Everyman's Library), p. 52.
18. Frederick Engels, *Anti-Dühring* (International Publishers), pp. 345-46 (italics added). Cf. Marx, *Capital*, vol. I (Modern Library), p. 92.
19. Sidney Hook, *Slavic Review*, vol. XXI, no. 3 (September 1962), p. 553.

total regeneration of man. At the same time we are sympathetic to Hook's criticism of Tucker's interpretation of Marxian alienation.

The problem preventing any reconciliation between the Hook and Tucker positions is that the discussion of alienation has been in terms of concepts that deal with alienation from the personal standpoint, suggesting that man possesses some innate human nature, whereas Marx said that "the nature of individuals thus depends on the material conditions determining their production."[20] Marx's concept of alienation is materialistic. He would ridicule current psychological interpretations of alienation just as in *The Communist Manifesto* he ridiculed "idealistic" (Hegelian and Feuerbachian) concepts of alienation. Bell is correct, if he means by "alienation" an "idealistic" concept of alienation, when he writes that "the historical Marx had in effect repudiated the idea of alienation. The term, because of its Hegelian overtones, was, for him, too abstract. And, because it carried psychological echoes of ideas such as 'man's condition,' it was too 'idealistic.' "[21] This is, in fact, Hook's critique of Tucker, a critique that is to the point given that Tucker treats Marxian alienation in "idealistic" terms.[22]

In Tucker's interpretation of Marx, the source of alienation is in "acquisitive fanaticism" or greed: "The compulsion that transforms free creative activity into alienated labor is the compulsion to amass wealth."[23] Man is "alienated by the inhuman force of money-worship."[24] "The acquisitive striving is the force that turns man's creative activity into compulsive alienated labor and depersonalizes him. It is the ground and source of his alienation from himself."[25] Throughout, Tucker interprets Marxian alienation as a "self-process" whereby man, under the domination of egoistic need, externalizes his productive power in the form of money. He writes that the "drama at the heart of *Capital* is, in its latent content, a drama of the inner life of man, of the self in conflict with itself. It is a representation of man being dehumanized and destroyed by a tyrannical force of acquisitiveness that has arisen and grown autonomous within him."[26]

20. Marx, *German Ideology*, p. 7.
21. Daniel Bell, *The End of Ideology* (Glencoe: The Free Press, 1960), p. 344.
22. Sidney Hook, "Marxism in the Western World" in *Marxist Ideology in the Contemporary World*, edited by M. Drachkovitch (New York: Praeger, 1966), pp. 26-27; see also Hook, *Slavic Review*, vol. XXI, pp. 552-53 and vol. XXII, pp. 189-90.
23. Robert Tucker, *Philosophy and Myth in Karl Marx* (Cambridge: Cambridge University Press, 1961), pp. 137-38.
24. Ibid., p. 140.   25. Ibid., p. 143.   26. Ibid., p. 215.

The source of Marxian alienation is not in the individual's psychology. By discussing alienation as a psychiatric phenomenon, Tucker fails to reconcile his emphasis on alienation with historical materialism; and it is here that his effort at reinterpretation founders. Tucker does not seem to be aware of the necessity to reconcile the concept of alienation with the concept of historical materialism. He writes that Marx "does not consider himself to be dealing with a psychiatric phenomenon. He regards himself as engaged in a criticism of political economy and believes that he has grasped and analyzed a fact of the economic life per se."[27] That Tucker thinks Marx went astray in his handling of alienation is obvious when he concludes that Marx was not justified in "conceiving the alienated self-relation as a social phenomenon in its essential nature. The intra-personal situation inescapably remains the primary fact, and the alienated social relation is only a derivative fact and a result."[28] Here Tucker fell into the error of criticizing Marx's concept of alienation from the standpoint of clinical psychology rather than interpreting Marx.[29]

As a result, Tucker's effort to find alienation in Capital strikes one as forced, to say the least. He must resort to arguing that the concept of "capital" in Capital is the name given to "what he [Marx] had called in the manuscripts a passion of greed"[30] and that the splitting of the alienated person's personality takes the form of the splitting of humanity into warring classes of workers and capitalists: "The war of self-alienated Marxian man with himself has become a class war across the battlefield of society."[31] Tucker fails to realize that money worship (and any other psychological condition) is a derivative, not a determinant in Marx's system. Greed or money worship cannot be the source of Marxian alienation but, at most, a condition socialized into man by the ideological superstructure resulting from the commodity mode of production.

Our interpretation of Marxian alienation vindicates the general position held by Tucker and others by vindicating Hook's criticism of Tucker. As Stigler has stated: "The test of an interpretation is its consistency with the main analytical conclusions of the system of thought under considera-

27. Ibid., p. 145.   28. Ibid., p. 149.
29. If Marxian alienation is a purely subjective phenomenon, then presumably it can be cured on the psychiatrist's couch and the function of the revolution vanishes.
30. Tucker, Philosophy and Myth in Karl Marx, p. 213.
31. Ibid., p. 146.

tion."[32] Tucker's interpretation of the source of Marxian alienation does not meet this test, but that only eliminates Tucker's interpretation of the source of Marxian alienation, not the thesis that the overcoming of alienation is the central theme of Marx. Our interpretation of Marxian alienation is consistent with historical materialism and accounts for the uniqueness of Marxian alienation to capitalism.

32. George Stigler, "Textual Exegesis as a Scientific Problem," *Economica*, New Series, vol. XXXII, no. 128 (November 1965), p. 448.

Index

Alienation: 1-18, 109-17 passim; commodity production as source of, 2, 9, 109-17; psychological and sociological approaches, 2; Marx's discontinued use of term, 2n; and materialist conception of history, 2-3; aspects of, 3, 7; Marx's mature treatment of, 6; and economic scarcity, 6n; manifested in contradictions in commodities, 8-9; psychological and sociological features of, 9, 116; as product of market system, 10; as rationale for Marx's hatred of capitalism, 10n; transcendence of, 10; and central planning, 10-14, 59-61, 114; and Marx's classification of economic systems, 15; private property as source of, 109-11; division of labor as source of, 109-13, 112n; of capitalist, 113; greed as source of, 114-17; as central theme of Marx, 114, 117; idealistic conception of, 115-16; materialistic conception of, 115-16; and historical materialism, 115-17

Ames, Edward, 73-74
Anderson, Thornton, 20
Arnold, Arthur Z., 21n
Authority, 57-58
Averitt, Robert T., 51n

Bajt, Alexander, 107
Balassa, Bela, 104
Banks, nationalization of, 29
Barone, Enrico, 99-100, 101
Bator, F., 100n
Beckmann, Martin J., 58
Bell, Daniel, 109-10, 115
Bergson, Abram, 74, 89, 91n, 92

Bognar, Jozsef, 83
Bolsheviks, Marxian aspirations of, 1, 21n, 47
Brest-Litovsk Treaty, 30
Brutzkus, Boris, 21n, 22, 44
Buchanan, James M., 53n, 96n
Bukharin, Nikolai, 13, 90n, 101, 107

Campbell, Robert, 48, 73
Capitalism: defined organizationally by Marx, 17; uniqueness of, 114
Capital market, polycentric form under public ownership, 79
Carr, E. H., 22-25
Cash nexus, 18
Central planners, as supply agents, 71, 79, 80
Central planning: aim of, 57, 60-61; problem of, 75, 66-69; as determination of new investment, 79; as piecemeal intervention, 80
Central planning board, as redundant entity in Lange's model, 94-96
Central plans, as forecasts, 78
Collective farm production, as commodity production, 46-47, 87
Commodities: fetishism of, 5; veil of, 5; characteristics of labor that produces commodities, 7; and alienated labor, 5, 7, 9; antithesis and contradictions in, 7-9; defined by Marx, 111-12
Commodity: Marx's definition of, 4; money form of, 5; fetishism, 6-7
Commodity production: 15-18, 60, 81, 84, 85-88, 91, 92; as source of alienation, 2, 9, 109-17; contradictions in,

PAUL CRAIG ROBERTS holds the William E. Simon Chair in Political Economy at the Center for Strategic and International Studies in Washington, D.C., and is Senior Research Fellow at the Hoover Institution, Stanford University. Dr. Roberts received his B.S. from the Georgia Institute of Technology, his Ph.D. in economics from the University of Virginia, and has done post-graduate work at the University of California at Berkeley and at Oxford University. He was an exchange student to the Soviet Union in 1961.

Dr. Roberts worked during 1975–78 on the Congressional staff, where he drafted the Kemp-Roth bill and played a leading role in developing bipartisan support for a supply-side economic policy. During 1981–82, he served as Assistant Secretary of the Treasury for Economic Policy. In 1987 the French government, recognizing him as "the artisan of a renewal in economic science and policy after half a century of state interventionism," awarded him the Legion of Honor.

Dr. Roberts is the author of *The Supply-Side Revolution* (1984) and *Marx's Theory of Exchange, Alienation, and Crisis* (with Matthew A. Stephenson, 1973), and a contributor to numerous professional journals. A former editor and columnist for the *Wall Street Journal*, he is currently a columnist for *Business Week*, the Scripps Howard News Service, and the *Washington Times*, as well as a frequent contributor to the *Wall Street Journal* and the *Los Angeles Times*.